P9-DMI-054

PRAISE FOR *THE TROUBLE WITH MEN*

"I've often wondered whether a married person can write about sex and love with any degree of candor and hope to stay married. David Shields's answer: a book that is dangerously, melancholically truthful but also an elegant work of art. *The Trouble with Men* is unexpectedly moving and sneakily profound."

—Laura Kipnis

"I have long admired David Shields and his literary departures, but *The Trouble with Men* is a departure from the departures. I'm haunted by this book, also a little obsessed with it, confused by it, afraid of it, angry at it, in awe of it, thankful for it."

—Meghan Daum

"In an era of reckonings, *The Trouble with Men*, nearly gymnastic in structure, is a timely and trenchant book unlike anything I've read before: stabbing, with confessional and sharp-witted boldness, into big themes of sex and love and power."

—Cathy Alter

"*The Trouble with Men* is truly great, and I mean it—a great book such as no one has ever written. Montaigne and Rousseau are the clear predecessors, but they pulled their punches. Shields is riskier and more down-to-earth, his obsessiveness is on target, and he strikes home."

—Peter Brooks

"In our culture at this moment, the prevailing discussion of the way relationships work between groups and between individuals often leaves no space for contradiction. *The Trouble with Men* cuts deep, making the conversation more satisfyingly messy. It does this through lacerating self-examination and a complexly organized symphony of voices and sources (from scholarly to pop) circling one another, sometimes harmoniously and sometimes in conflict. I find the book more beautiful and affirmative in its confusion, self-doubt, and embarrassment than many of the (even well-intentioned) narratives about gender we're forcing down each other's throats right now."

—Elizabeth Cooperman

"The most original, insightful, and heartbreaking book about sexual desire since Roland Barthes's *A Lover's Discourse*. No contemporary writer writes with the honesty, ingenuity, and originality that David Shields brings to the notoriously slippery subject of erotic love. Devastating, inspiring, and totally enthralling."

—Clancy Martin

"Smart, ecstatic, subdued, clever, genuine, fearful, and brave, all at once. This is a beautiful book."

—Lisa Taddeo

"*Do I love you? Do you love me? What kind of marriage do we want? How real? Do you like me? Do you care about me? Are you in love with me? Do you love making love with me? Do you like being married to me? Do you love being married to me?* A playful, sneaky, rangy, pulsating, vertiginous, and invaluable investigation into these questions, which belong to all of us."

—Katherine Standefer

"Writers have always thrived on their conflicting impulses toward personal confession and universal significance. Shields exposes that conflict and pushes it to the limit. Readers will be electrified and frankly amazed, not so much by the completeness of the confession as the personal circumstances in which it is made. And amazed again when, in the space of a few lines, the personal and particular are submerged in a turbulent ocean of collective longing and frustration."

—Tim Parks

"In *The Trouble with Men*, when Shields pushes his own incisive shards up against those of dozens of other writers, the fragments touch upon one another in startling ways. The result is a poetic, unique, and powerful mosaic."

—Melanie Thernstrom

"I've read all of Shields's books, and this is my favorite: the most genuinely vulnerable thing he has written. That said, the vulnerability isn't maudlin or grotesque; it sneaks through, though it's unmistakably there. And the self-reflexive gestures (the way in which he's interrogating the book even as he's composing it) are more powerful than ever here. I love the humor in concert with the wide-open danger. It's as though he's troubled by the material and trying to know the material but not know it *too* well. There were moments in the last third when I had to stand up because I couldn't read it sitting down."

—Peter Mountford

"The most boldly naked book I've ever read."

—Matthew Vollmer

21ST CENTURY ESSAYS

David Lazar and Patrick Madden, Series Editors

THE TROUBLE WITH MEN

REFLECTIONS ON SEX, LOVE, MARRIAGE, PORN, AND POWER

DAVID SHIELDS

MAD CREEK BOOKS, AN IMPRINT OF
THE OHIO STATE UNIVERSITY PRESS
COLUMBUS

9980

Library of Congress Cataloging-in-Publication Data
Names: Shields, David, 1956– author.
Title: The trouble with men : reflections on sex, love, marriage, porn, and power /
    David Shields.
Other titles: 21st century essays.
Description: Columbus : Mad Creek Books, an imprint of The Ohio State
    University Press, [2019] | Series: 21st century essays
Identifiers: LCCN 2018039364 | ISBN 9780814255193 (pbk. ; alk. paper) | ISBN
    0814255191 (pbk. ; alk. paper)
Subjects: LCSH: Shields, David, 1956– | Sex. | Love. | Marriage. | Masochism.
Classification: LCC PS3569.H4834 A6 2019 | DDC 814/.54—dc23
LC record available at https://lccn.loc.gov/2018039364

Cover design by Jeff Clark
Text design by Juliet Williams
Type set in Adobe Caslon

The author expresses his sincere and profound gratitude to the Atlantic Center for the Arts for the Pabst Endowed Chair Residency Fellowship, the Frye Art Museum/Artist Trust Consortium for the James W. Ray Distinguished Artist Award, the Pollock Endowment for the Loren D. Milliman Professorship, and the Royalty Research Fund for a study grant.

A note on the text: A bracketed name at the end of a paragraph indicates a direct quotation or a close paraphrase of something someone else has written or said.

CONTENTS

Everything is about sex except sex. Sex is about power.
—*Robert Michels*

I
—

LET'S SAY

I'M WRITING

A LOVE LETTER

TO YOU

Many years ago I read, with deepening fervor, installments of my graduate student Michael Jarmer's novel about a foot fetishist, who says, "I turned the volume all the way down so I could concentrate on the images before me: the shoes holding the squirming victim down, the heels threatening harm, the feet disrobed, deshoed, desocked, destockinged, the foot in the mouth, both naked feet in the groin, the cum shot between the toes, the whole nine yards." Feet have never been my thing, but reading Michael's manuscript ignited something in me. I would think it would be somewhat analogous to realizing, midway through one's life, that one is gay.

In dozens of complex, various, and subtle ways, you seem to me, subtly, sadistic; I am, perhaps not quite so subtly, masochistic. This tinge is there as an undercurrent—an odd, unspoken tug—in our relationship (in our sexual relationship in particular). It's there as a shadow of something strange and mysterious and deep.

*

This book aims to be a short, intensive immersion into the perils, limits, and possibilities of human intimacy.

How did I get this way? What is this way? Our marriage involving this way. Attempt to stop being this way. Implications of being this way.

Or: What is it like to be this way? How did I get this way? What is it like for you that I'm this way? Can I live with being this way? Can I stop being this way?

Or: Hamartia; childhood; marital strife; irreparable damage; ah, but we are all like this.

Or: The nature of; the sources of; our marriage involving; my attempts to rid myself of; a partial defense of.

Or: Human history of; psychic sources of; our marriage involving; attempt to eliminate and/or suppress and/or attempt to disentangle from (and/or affirm?); psychological/philosophical implications of, etc.

Or: How 1) one is wounded; 2) one tries to overcome these wounds; 3) these wounds become the very theater of one's self; 4) one despairs that one will ever overcome those wounds, and these wounds lead one to anger/violence; and 5) finally, we connect to other people by realizing we are all wounded (this is our scar tissue and our glue, etc.).

Or: The nature of masochism. The origins of masochism. Our marriage involving masochism. Attempt to surmount masochism. A philosophy (and/or a psychology?) of masochism.

Or: Acknowledgment of my masochistic tendencies. Biological, psychological, and philosophical sources. Manifestation in our marriage. The sense that all there is in the author's life/heart is suffering. The sense that, for all human beings, existence is suffering.

Or: *On Being One's Own Bitch.*

*

Perhaps the real subject is my willingness, or at least desire/impulse, to write this book, to risk our marriage—

Do I love you?

Do you love me?

What kind of marriage do we want?

How real?

Or: Do you like me?
Do you care about me?

Or: Are you in love with me?
Do you like making love with me?
Do you love making love with me?

(Don't answer.)

*

The agon, then: [Lawrence Durrell]
  What is it then between us? [Walt Whitman]

  What separates us?
  How did we get here?
  What went wrong?
  What do we do now?
  Is there any way past except through?

History in one corner and Love in the other? Fine. Ring the bell. Let the fight begin. Love, he thinks, will bring history to its knees. [Scott Spencer]
Romance holds my attention only if it promises a sizable element of risk. [Edwin Dobb]

*

Aristotle's theory of dramatic structure (introduction, rising action, climax, falling action, dénouement) is nothing more or less than a diagram of the sexual act. It doesn't mean the theory's true, and it doesn't mean it isn't true. It just means sex is everything.

Some people don't like sex, some people like sex but don't see it as an especially important part of their life, and some people see sex as a journey. It's never been a minor part of my life, even when we were hardly ever having sex.

I've never written by hand or in bed before, but I'm writing all of this with a pen on a legal pad, lying down.

*

I collaborated with your cousin Samantha on a book, *That Thing You Do with Your Mouth*, about sex and power and the pleasure principle and repetition compulsion (as a child, she was abused by her stepbrothers; as an adult, she briefly dubbed Italian porn into English and in most of her relationships has sought out the infliction and receipt of harm)— which I hoped would satiate my interest in the subject but only sharpened my appetite to explore the matter further, in and for myself.

"Treatment" for "opening out" that book into a movie:

Plot Point A. Having been formatted by traumas in his past, Alan believes he's overcome these things and now has the wisdom and experience to help Michelle deal with her traumas in the same way that he's dealt with his: by writing a book.

Reversal. Alan hasn't overcome his issues to the extent that he thought he had; he grasps that he's using Michelle and her story to guide him through his own past, and he sees her as a sort of muse—a way to get to the story he really wants to write: his own.

Plot Point B. In what seems to be a mixture of genuine admiration, a desperate need to know that despite his issues he's still desirable, and a "safe" way to explore flirtation outside of his marriage (he knows that a relationship with Michelle is not actually feasible), Alan professes his love to her.

Gloom. Alan's high (unrealistic?) expectations for Michelle and himself cause the project to implode and Alan to face failure.

Finale. Michelle is able to achieve an emotional catharsis, but Alan realizes it wasn't his support and guidance that led her there; he finds that he was always as fucked up as she was, and they're both as fucked up as everyone else. Michelle leaves with satisfaction in that knowledge, but Alan has opened a wound in himself that he now must deal with.

Memo to would-be producers of the would-be film version:
The main way the film would fail would be if it wound up illustrating a Freudian map: Michelle ceaselessly replays the abuse; Alan is defined by his stutter, his relationship to his mother, etc. Those shadows are clearly there, but I think a better way to approach the material is this: due to each of their backgrounds, Michelle and Alan can't see each other and others except as figures of their own psychic projection. I would argue that this is true of any human being, and I would also argue that the ability of any human being to get past such phantasms is very limited. In a more sentimental version of the film, each of them would come to see the other as real. In our version, something else happens:
Michelle has a somewhat therapeutic relationship to her own pain; by the end of the film, she comes to a more philosophic view: We're all messed up; so am I. And there's solace in that. She sees a little beyond herself. Whereas Alan is an expert on everyone else's pain except his own. He has a tragic, "philosophic" view of pain, but when he's confronted with his own psychic confusion/needs, he has trouble holding onto the tragic view and in a way yearns for a more therapeutic vision: Heal me, now.
Michelle sees her own iciness as brokenness, whereas Alan somewhat madly persists in seeing it as sexy distance. By film's end, does he finally get this? Maybe. Maybe not.

Are illusions better than nothing? Can we sustain ourselves on dream crumbs? What else can we do? What else are there but dreams, phantoms, and other people? [Hilton Als]

*

Let's say I'm writing a love letter to you. I'm just trying to be as truthful as possible. I'm not thinking, How is it going to affect you? Ultimately, of course, I'm aware of trying to create an intimate connection between you and me, but in a way it's the last thing on my mind.

It's so perfect that you don't want me to write this book (because you don't want to read it); therefore, I have to write it. So, too, if you were fine with me writing it, I'd have no desire to write it.

—knowing how boring this book would be if you were willing for it to be written (if, for instance, you were Catherine Millet); it's your unwillingness to sanction it that makes it necessary.

You, my darling, are the perfect muse, a ceaseless spur; I truly love how little you like any of my books—including this one? Maybe you'll love this one. Maybe you'll hate it. (How do you share an entire life with someone who feels the way she does about your work, Whitney Otto asked me, and is this only about the work?) The only reason it's being written—or at least one of the main reasons it's being written, the reason I started writing it—is to talk, finally, to you.

Or: I still don't know you at all; hence this letter.

(It would be such a relief to be honest, for once. I'm dying for everything to get out in the open, but it never does.)

Or: This letter has slept so long at the bottom of my gym bag that it seems less like a message than an artifact. Perhaps that's why I put it to sleep in the first place. Even while writing it, it seemed to belong to the ancient past or, more exactly, to another lost day in this lonesome city. I'll send it along, though, because I can't really remedy my old impressions.

A letter always arrives at its destination. [Barbara Johnson]

Beware what you say, you say to me. *It has a way of getting found out.*

Or: Idea for a novel—

A husband and wife talk to each other for the entire night about their sexual fantasies.

When, many years ago, I presented this idea to a literary agent and explained that I wasn't sure I could imagine my way into the woman's half of the dialogue, the agent pushed her chair back, uncrossed her legs, and said, "If you want, I'll be her for you." I'll never forgive myself for not getting down on my hands and knees and crawling across the floor to her.

I remember saying once, I can't understand these chaps who go round American universities explaining how they write poems; it's like going round explaining how you sleep with your wife. Whoever I was talking to said, "They'd do that, too, if their agents could fix it." [Philip Larkin]

Intimacy holds the fascination of a car wreck, the sickening promise of voyeurism. Can the author possibly realize just how much he betrays of his life, his psyche? The content of the "novel" is so clearly and completely drawn from the author's experience that although *Intimacy* was published as fiction, it was received—venomously—as fact. [Kathryn Harrison]

—that whole question of what it means to set another person before the camera, trying to extract something of his or her soul. When are we exploiting? When are we caressing? Are they, maybe, the same? Maybe it's impossible not to do both. Maybe that's the truth of human relationships. [Ross McElwee]

If there's one word about me in the book, I'll never speak to you again.

Really—one word? Just one?

The threat this poses to your marriage is what worries me. Is it a masochistic book because it might cost you your marriage? I'd say it ain't worth that. [Otto]

*

My worst fear is to be held captive by niceness. What will I allow myself to say?

What is there to confess? Have I done something wrong? Yes. No. Circle one. Go ahead. Write on my manuscript. [Jarmer]

You thought you could hide behind your laptop, poor baby.

He had managed to take every struggle in his life and turn it into a form of sense save for this last one, which, being rooted in the senselessness of sexual desire, ended, for him, in shame. [Adam Gopnik]

Life is unfair—kill yourself or get over it. [Luke Haines and John Moore]

This book is an attempt to get over it.

*

In Jonathan Lethem's novel *You Don't Love Me Yet*, Carl, "the complainer," says about Matthew, the lead singer of a band, "There's nothing's sadder than being a genius of sex: evoking nothing but pleasure in the eyes of others."

And yet Carl, when confronted with his appetite for fame, says he wants only "what we all want—to move certain parts of the interior of myself into the external world, to see if they can be embraced."

At sixty-two, I have a different view of sex than I had at forty-two or fifty-two. I'm obsessed with it, but a lot of what I want to do is think about it.

Or: I'd like to attempt to understand our marriage (marriage as a genre?) better.

To me, it's a really interesting question, to say the least—what makes a marriage so difficult that it needs to be abandoned, and what is just usual M/F friction?

That is:

Do we want to stay together?

Why?

Why not?

The entire book is a wound. Even when its rhythm expresses the throb of pleasure, the pleasure is so ardent that it lays waste the personality experiencing it. [Brigid Brophy]

With all the "memoirs" being written that are naive victim narratives, I thought it might be useful to write a book that tries to ask interesting questions about pain rather than simply invoking it as a badge.

Originally, I tried to do a version of this book by having an email exchange with my writer-friend Brenda Phillips, but the gulf was simply too wide: she's so much better looking than I am—and as a result has had so many more sexual experiences—that we had next to nothing to talk about.

I'd always envisioned this book as an exploration of something about myself that I don't understand, and my confusion is interesting to me. There's nothing (no drive) more powerful than sex, although my closest high school friend (who wound up dying from a heroin overdose) once told me he'd rather have the best drug ever than the best pussy ever.

Someone—not sure who—once said (and I love this, even though I can count on one hand the number of times I've been high), "I trust drug people more than I trust anyone else, because you can't become one without desperation and self-hatred. Those are feelings that I understand, that make sense to me. We trust the people we understand."

One's own sexuality, for the most part, is a secret. We share bits and pieces with others, but not ever everything. In my experience, women are pretty uptight when it comes to talking about sex. I have very few women friends who are willing to "go there," and these women are fairly, as we used to say, oversexed. I have a friend who confessed that at a certain point in her life she was always masturbating in public— while driving in her car, in the library bathroom, and so on. Another friend gave her students blow jobs in her office. At the time, I was very turned on by these confessions. [Phillips]

The conventional wisdom among men is that women talk all the time about sex, with great specificity. I'm sure it varies, of course, from woman to woman and group to group—by class, education level, milieu, etc. It was surprising to me (and weirdly reassuring) when Brenda said that women talk about sex far less than advertised.

This should, of course, be a conversation I actually have with you. . . .

You're frightened that you're going to see yourself there. Or that you're going to find out what your husband/dad/ lover/friend thinks about you that's different from what you think about yourself. Or that you're going to find out something about your spouse/child/parent you don't want to know. Or worst of all that you're going to like it. [Sallie Tisdale]

*

My blurb for Jay Ponteri's memoir *Wedlocked* (pre-echo as self-flattery?):

Many recent books have been written, of course, about sex, love, marriage, men and women. Very few if any display the degree of intimacy, candor, and rawness that this book does. Very few if any so exactingly expose the male psyche. None that I can think of is smarter about the uses of fantasy.

My suggestion to Ponteri while he was writing it (misdirected advice to myself):

The book has to be willing to undermine you, wrest you from your fantasies, so that women emerge on top, as it were, of your fantasies. The work has to be about sexual fantasy and can't be sexual fantasy.

Otto's email to me about *Wedlocked* (redirected cautionary tale):

I'm three-quarters through and I will say that I believe I get it. It appears deceptively straightforward while it's anything but; it has genuine complexity. It isn't exactly about his shitty marriage, and it is about his shitty marriage. I get that Frannie is a figment and a stand-in (she is also someone he knows?), not just for all those women he can't have, but is a sort of personification of the core trouble with his marriage—and, by extension, the core trouble with marriage itself. I understand that this book is very much about his depression, his self-proclaimed misery and "brokenness," and the book's repetition mimics the ennui and circularity of depression. I love how he goes on a lengthy riff about not wanting to hurt people, trying to avoid it all the time, while the act of writing this book is going to be hurtful to at least a few people (I'm thinking of his son, for one), and he does it anyway, because he's the most important person in his world. I'm not making a judgment about that; it's more of an observation. Part of the problem I'm having is that the book feels a little mired—which, again, I think is part of the point—but it's hard to write about being mired without the book itself becoming kind of a slog. Even his refusal to paragraph, laying down dense blocks of text, visually keeps the reader (me) out of the book.

It's all him all the time. He talks (endlessly) about his wife's "anger" over his "rejection." He thinks that all her responses are connected to his "rejection of her," his "loss of love for her." He doesn't know the first thing about women. He has no inkling—none—of the magnitude of a woman's frustration or what they give up or what they long for and how deep it goes. (It's one thing to write candidly about the marriage and another to describe her soiled underwear.) It isn't that he doesn't get them; he doesn't seem to care to get them. On some level, they simply don't interest him. He's interested only in himself and how they factor into that self. His book is an authentic account—I'll give him that—but there's no air in the room. I can't enter this story. He fills every available crack and crevice, as it were, and is so busy telling on himself and anticipating what the reader (or his wife) may think that the reader has no space to think. I'm listening to a man who is pretending to ask me a question, then answering it for me, too.

*

Nicholson Baker's view of sexuality is curiously devoid of any notions of power or powerlessness, not to mention sadness, ambivalence, or emotion of any kind. As Janet Maslin has written, he "has a well-hidden prim streak, and he sticks to cheery little vignettes in which everybody gets hot but nobody gets hurt." (Remind me again—what world is that?) In *Vox,* the two (indistinguishable) characters' fantasy lives appear to be focused primarily on product placement; the fantasies have absolutely no psychic heat to them, and neither Abby nor Jim has the slightest tendency toward domination or submission. In *The Fermata,* Baker displays an utterly mechanistic, round-peg-goes-in the-round-hole view of romance. *House of Holes?* Dunno. Never read it. Only in America could a novelist who writes about sex as if it were a subset of the Shopping Channel be praised as the thinking person's pornographer.

And she—so tall, so splendid in the saddle, so fair! Yes, Leonora was extraordinarily fair and so extraordinarily the real thing that she seemed too good to be true. You don't, I mean, as a rule, get it all so superlatively together. To be the county family, to look the county family, to be so appropriately and perfectly wealthy; to be so perfect in manner—even just to the saving touch of insolence that seems to be necessary. [Ford Madox Ford]

> . . . the desire to subdue, which is normal and active,
> and the desire for suffering, which is not; . . . [Henri Cole]

A middle-aged midget in a double-breasted suit came down the alley, walked under one girl's dress, reached up to pull it over himself like a roof, and began to suck. The girl stood, looking at nothing. When the midget was finished, he slid her panties back up and spat onto the sidewalk. Then he reached into his wallet. [William Vollmann]

Although I know this passage is about something awful and sad, I must admit (am ashamed to admit) I find the midget's neediness and the girl's indifference thrilling.

*

Attempting to pick me up at a gym on the Upper West Side in 1983, Harold Brodkey told me that when Theodore Solotaroff published Brodkey's fifty-page novella "Innocence" in *American Review*, Solotaroff had zero comprehension of how or why it would take Wiley and his mouth all evening to bring Orra to climax.

—James Jones's claim that women don't enjoy sex; they enjoy being wanted; that's their pleasure. This is the expression on his part of pure fear, but some of it is generational.

—Philip Roth and his novels that, with few exceptions, ever really get to anything about sex. It's just sex. He rarely examines what his characters want from sex. To me, it's transparent how submissive he is ("Maybe the wisest solution for me is to live on all fours! Crawl through life feasting on pussy, and leave the righting of wrongs and the fathering of families to the upright creatures!"), but he doesn't have the nerve or will to investigate this.

So, too, Saul Bellow: "He saw twenty paces away the white soft face and independent look of a woman in a shining black straw hat . . . and eyes that even in the signal-dotted obscurity reached him with a force she could never be aware of. Those eyes might be blue, perhaps green, even gray—he would never know. . . . They expressed a sort of female arrogance which had an immediate sexual power over him; he experienced it again that very moment."

—Norman Mailer and his insane theories about the rectum and the devil and eternity.

Bernard Malamud's biographer, Philip Davis, refers to Malamud's "fantasy of a slavish sexuality, wildly close to masochism."

I don't see the point of privacy. [Brodkey]

The prison mantra "Do your own time" is a seductive slogan. I find that I quote it to myself occasionally, but really I don't subscribe to the sentiment. I'm not, after all, in prison. Stoicism is of no use to me whatsoever. What I'm a big believer in—apparently—is talking about everything until I'm blue in the face.

Gary Chapman writes about this phenomenon in his book *The Five Love Languages*, when he describes Babblers and Dead Seas. Babblers talk, Dead Seas listen, and the two types usually hook up. Chapman explains that Dead Seas keep everything in; they're fine not talking. On the other hand, Babblers feel compelled to yack about every vague and fleeting impression gained through their senses. As Chapman puts it, Babblers "have no reservoir." [Lulu Johnson]

Obviously, I'm a Babbler; just as obviously, you're a Dead Sea.

*

Jack and I are watching *Diamonds Are Forever*. Sean Connery questions a woman by the sea. Her response is flirtatious, inviting. He grabs her bathing suit and twists it around her neck. Jack likes to pin my arms when he makes love to me. I like it, too. [Alice Linker]

BEAT ME, FUCK ME, EAT ME, WHIP ME, CUM ON MY TITS, AND THEN GET THE FUCK OUT. [T-shirt worn by goth waitress at a bar in West Seattle]

In British and Hollywood casting-call terms, respectively, I fancy femmes fatales, but (to the extent anyone does) it's ingénues who fancy me.

It is precisely equality that destroys our libidos, equality that bores men and women alike. [Cristina Nehring]

What I'm interested in is the point at which people break and treat each other awfully. [Paula Hawkins]

What I'm interested in are the ways in which stories of suffering might be used to mask other, less marketable stories of suffering.

*

On my thirtieth birthday, under your influence, I got my left ear pierced and bought a diamond earring. I wore various earrings over the next ten years, but wearing an earring never really worked for me, and on my fortieth birthday, under the influence of our daughter, who thought it made me look like a pirate, I took out the earring I was then wearing—a gold hoop—and haven't worn an earring since. Earrings forced me to confront the nature of my style, or lack of style. I'm certainly not macho enough to wear an earring as if I were a tough guy, but neither am I effeminate enough to wear an earring in my right ear as if I were maybe gay-in-training. Instead, I'm just me, muddling through in the middle, and the earring forced me, over time, to see this, acknowledge it, and respond to it.

Pornography, Catharine MacKinnon writes, "eroticizes hierarchy"; it "makes inequality into sex, which makes it enjoyable, and into gender, which makes it seem natural." MacKinnon is saying that a man lying on top of a woman assumes that what excites her is the idea of her body being invaded by a phallic master. [Leo Bersani]

—the blue movie running pretty much nonstop in every man's mind.

A lot of feminists want to know: What do women want out of erotica? We want to see women coming. That's so far ahead of everything else on the list, it's hardly worth it to get into anything else. [Susie Bright]

The idol WOMEN DO IT FOR LOVE / MEN DO IT FOR JOY lies broken on the rug like a mutilated sex toy: it's orgasm, orgasm, orgasm. [Tanya Gold]

If you understand that Andrea Dworkin was the reincarnation of the Marquis de Sade, her whole thing makes sense. She was a severely repressed sadist. Read her novel *Fire and Ice* as a companion piece to Sade's *Justine,* and you'll realize they're exactly the same story: a woman tries to be virtuous, tries to do the right thing, and what happens? She gets fucked in the ass in a really mean way, over and over again. And when I read that Dworkin had a special place for dishes that her partner hadn't cleaned properly (so he could re-scrub them), I thought, This is all too clear. [Bright]

The greatest poverty is not to live / In a physical world, to feel that one's desire / Is too difficult to tell from despair. [Wallace Stevens]

Am I seeking pain by watching these videos, trying to re-live that darkness because it's the only thing that feels really real? [Samantha Matthews]

There are about forty-nine masochists to one sadist. [Cyril Connolly]

My astonishing victory over Menti did not give me a pleasure one-hundredth part as intense as the pain she gave me when she left me for M. de Rospiec. [Stendahl]

In my book, it's the losers who are the true winners. [Tony Sheehan]

Win forever. [Pete Carroll]

Pornography is not, in my experience and opinion, a sub-stitute for closeness; it's a revel in distance.

It's an eros of disconnection (Chris Rock says his porn addiction made him "sexually autistic").

What I like about porn is its descent into hell.

*

I admired Tisdale's *Talk Dirty to Me* more before she told me, "You have no idea what I didn't include." I could then tell how much the book wanted to be about her masochism, and I could also see how little she had really explored her sexual psyche—in fact, how thoroughly she had evaded talk-ing about it.

If someone were to call me "cunt," en passant, I would be irritated and upset. So, too, if someone tried to woo me with such talk. But on the way to arousal, ooh la la. The only sex I remember the actual moments of—the lighting, me, him, the feeling of the fucking—was with this guy I could take or leave, in a way, but who that night murmured "cunt" in the middle of hammering into me. Thus was born my love for dirty talk during sex. [Phillips]

Tisdale, to me: It was just another challenging subject to me, but the rest of the world thinks it's something special. Are you sure you're up for that? And your wife?

James Joyce's wife, Nora, said that she wished he'd write "nice" stories. I think it must be built into every writer's marriage that the spouse can't see the work the way the writer has to. (With the entirely spurious exception of Vladimir and Véra Nabokov's marriage, which seems to me to have been an air-conditioned nightmare.) I wonder, too, if there isn't built into domestic interplay a certain need for mystery, or difference, between the spouses that makes it almost necessary for one spouse not to understand the other's writing, particularly when the writing touches on their life together. (If they were ever to completely understand each other, would that mean the marriage was over?)

*

Nabokov is understood to possess Olympian distance on Humbert, but actually he has almost none. I like Alfred Appel's annotations to *Lolita*, but I can't read the book anymore, can you? All that preening is just an embarrassment now, don't you think?

Nic Kelman's novel *Girls* is reminiscent of *Lolita*. Kelman addresses this, arguing that Humbert isn't really a pedophile, since Lolita has already reached adolescence by the time he seduces her. Kelman has a go at Nabokov for his cowardice. It's a crucial move, addressing the reader's inevitable association of *Girls* with *Lolita* and airily dismissing the latter. Kelman is alerting the reader to the fact that unlike Nabokov or indeed Humbert, he's not fucking around. It's one of the many ways he does everything he can to shake the reader down. While having sex with an underage prostitute, the protagonist tells himself that she enjoys her job so much because she was probably molested throughout her childhood. Frequently, the reader finds himself "allowing" a completely immoral choice in order to read more about it.

Last night, in the smoking-room at Princess Mathilde's, the conversation turned to Rossini. We talked of his priapism and his taste, in the matter of love, for unwholesome practices and then of the strange and innocent pleasures the old composer took in his final years. He would get young girls to undress to the waist, and while his hands wandered lasciviously over their torsos, he would give the end of his little finger to suck. [Edmond and Jules de Goncourt]

—Lionel Trilling's ludicrous notion that *Lolita* is ultimately "not about sex but about love."

Email to Brenda: In my mind, I usually separate sex and love; in fact, where they meet is problematic for me sometimes. When I get a really big crush on someone, I usually have romantic fantasies rather than sexual ones. It takes a while for the lust to kick in. On the other hand, I'm perfectly capable of being extremely lustful toward those I'm not romantically interested in. I suppose if we go ahead with this, we're bound to run into each other's pathologies. . . .

*

In her advice column in the *Seattle Times,* cultural anthropologist Jennifer James explains that "women used to be attracted to big men because they could bring home meat and defend us against marauders," but "women are less likely to be battered by small partners," so she encourages her readers to "reverse the current genetic trend and save the universe" by marrying "thoughtful little people."

Sometimes I think men are clever, too, and give out that they're defeated for the sake of peace. This—unless we explain it by masochism—would account for the large amount of man-made and man-read literature on the subject of the humiliated male. [E. M. Forster]

Combative until I meet resistance, I then become conciliatory. [Simon Gray]

I don't remember what will help me; I remember what hurt. [Samantha Hunt]

My primary interest in SM is in hurting people. [Pat Califia]

I can't imagine what it feels like to humiliate another person. I've always identified with the person beaten down. I still do.

Even when, throughout my twenties, I would break up with someone, I would later contrive to seek her friendship, thereby assuring that ultimately she would reject me.

*

Everybody needs someone to beat up, and the East Coast defines itself as the East Coast by caricaturing the West Coast, which I didn't really understand until I moved back to the West Coast (I grew up in LA and San Francisco, lived on the East Coast for two decades, and have now lived in Seattle for twenty-five years). It's simple but true: power is a fulcrum. East/west; north/south; white/black; male/female.

Group X always needs Group Y to buff its own sense of superiority. We are mind-haunted civilization; you are the physical beauty we'll contemplate. In this view, the West is in a perpetual state of nature.

The West is invariably referred to as "out West," as a way to underscore the idea that the Northeast is the center of American "culture" (it no longer is; the locus of all innovation is now here—I don't sound defensive at all, do I?). China/Japan; Japan/Korea; Athens/Rome; Christendom/the Roman Empire; London/New York—every society has forever condescended to every society that followed afterward.

—the inherent and apparently irreparable masochism, for me, of life in Seattle; the abstraction of "New York" brandished (by the "media" but also, obviously, by myself) as an endless cudgel.

A suspension bridge outside Seattle wags in the wind like the tail of a near-death golden retriever trapped in a stranded commuter car halfway between two shores. [Hunt]

I always root for the underdog; I literally can't comprehend how anyone could root for anyone else.

I check the Mariners score on my phone, hoping they've won but needing them to lose.

The better story always comes from the losing locker room. [Ben Maller]

*

I love "losers," e.g., LeBron.
I hate "winners," e.g., Jordan.

I love "termite art," e.g., Wallace.
I hate "white elephant art," e.g., Franzen.

—E. B. White's notion that one shouldn't move to New York unless one is willing to be lucky. During the 1980s I lived in and around New York for eight years, on and off, and remained adamantly unwilling to be lucky.

Which, of course, is part of why I hate it so much, its relentlessly self-regarding triumphalism.

Lucinda Williams: I fucking hate fucking New York.

The idiocy of New York can forge the strongest individuals, but it can also destroy them and drive them mad. [Simon Critchley]

American cinema loves outcasts, rebels, and misfits, but above all it values winners. Mr. Brando was always bored with winning and pushed his art, as far as he could, in the other direction. [A. O. Scott]

He gave us a botched career in the end. [James Harvey]

Ice-T is the only person who does things that completely jeopardize his career just to stay awake. [Chuck D]

—the eros of being judged inadequate (in *A Moveable Feast*, F. Scott Fitzgerald asks Hemingway, in a pissoir, if, as Zelda claims, his dick is too small and is assured by Papa that he's "perfectly fine—you look at yourself from above and you look foreshortened"; Hem then takes Scott to the Louvre to demonstrate the point).

—the authority of "success" (Hemingway) vs. the authority of "failure" (Fitzgerald).

The Crack-Up matters more to me than all of Hemingway, all of Faulkner, and the rest of Fitzgerald.

*

Throughout various books, I've quoted and "misquoted" hundreds of sentences, without "proper" attribution—in order to advance a particular literary, aesthetic, and philosophical principle but also as a way to be "bad" and get spanked (for being bad)?

The first time a man ever spanked me in sex, I had an orgasm and I remember thinking, Oh my god! I pulled myself up in a very pristine way and said, "Don't you ever do that again" and made this little note to myself that "he was probably mentally ill." This was after my orgasm. Now I'm embarrassed. I wish I could write him a thank-you letter now: "I'm sorry. I was so wrong. You were so right." [Bright]

There is probably little connection between a man's sexual obsessions and his political inclinations. Think of Kenneth Tynan, a theater critic of the sixties and seventies, a prominent supporter of all left-wing and libertarian causes, who devoted the last decade of his life to spanking women, thinking about spanking women, brooding endlessly about spanking women. [Gray]

This is completely wrong. How could the two not be knitted together? Many men who are viewed as having arrived at a position of cultural authority (e.g., Dick Morris, Rex Ryan, J. D. Salinger) develop/unveil foot fetishes, as a way to evacuate their hard-won authority.

—authoritarians and their not-so-secret fantasies of being fucked/fucked over/fucked up the ass.

Conventional political wisdom:
Democrats fall in love.
Republicans fall in line.

Drill, baby, drill. [Sarah Palin]

—your uncanny ability to frame and phrase resentment as quasi-cheerfulness.

*

In the marketplace, at least, rape is the natural order of things and remarkably popular, too, on both sides of the exchange. People hand over their money, their lives, to DynaZauber or any other corporation; they know what they're getting. They want to get connected. The customers are always bottoms looking to get topped, the harder and bloodier, the better. [K. W. Jeter]

I was raped by a doctor—which is, you know, so bittersweet for a Jewish girl. [Sarah Silverman]

She tells of a night at Diamond Lil's on Canal Street, where "Viva's sitting onstage, her legs spread wide." While her customer is buried and busy, she holds a cigarette in one hand, a drink in the other, and chitchats with a girlfriend about another girlfriend. "Every two minutes or so Viva taps him on the head and he hands her a 20 from a stack of bills he's holding, never looking up." [Toni Bentley's discussion of Jodi Sh. Doff essay]

One online dominatrix pooh-poohs all the knowing talk of the "natural power" of a domme making a "proud man" stoop—you know, the lawyer, doctor, or judge who wants to clean toilets on a leash. "What we talk about, often off the internet and out of leather, is the power of money. More often than not the money tops the scene. The biggest trick is really coming to terms with the fact that money is the boss's boss." [Bentley's discussion of Sadie Lune essay]

I admire the authority of being on one's knees in front of the event. [Brodkey]

—kneeling with my hands behind me but without any ropes, a willing prisoner . . .

Look at the names and photos of Nicole Brown Simpson's mother and sisters Denise, Tanya, and Dominique: all *belles dames sans merci.*

Look at photos of her father: classic submissive.

O. J. killed Nicole because they had an overtly SM relationship—she was his slave, and she eased out of the chains.

This is the only story of mine whose moral I know. I don't think it's a marvelous moral; I simply happen to know what it is: [Kurt Vonnegut]

The leash lasts longer than the hand that releases it. [Ponteri]

In other words—
How did I wash up on this shore?
What wrong road took me here?

II
———

THE FOUR

PEOPLE IN

EVERY

BEDROOM

I can't understand where all this misery comes from; I'm not sophisticated enough to tell you that it comes, simply enough, from inside me.

—attuned exclusively to the earthquake of loss.

In *Peter and the Wolf,* the duck is melancholic—accustomed to and designed for loss—so we know well before it happens that he's destined to be sacrificed to the wolf. [Robert Clark]

This is known as catastrophizing. Catastrophizing isn't a healthy or successful coping strategy. [Denise Mann]

I'm in thrall to a pathos that has ruled my life since I was very young.

We're going to need a forensics team. . . .

*

A newborn baby makes the transition from a comfortable, fluid-filled environment to a cold, air-filled one by creating a suction fifty times stronger than the average adult breath. I was a breech birth, the danger of which is that the head comes out last, which dramatically increases the possibility that the umbilical cord will get wrapped around the neck (in this case, my neck). I entered the world feet first, then remained in the hospital an extra week to get a little R&R in a warm incubator, which my father guarded like a goalie whenever anyone came within striking distance. If I laid still for more than a few minutes, he reportedly pounded on the glass dome. I wasn't dead, Dad. I was only sleeping. All my life I've told myself I sought a cold, air-filled environment (danger), but really what I'm drawn to is that comfortable, fluid-filled environment (safety).

As silly as this may sound, I think being placed in an incubator has affected my sense of life as being exceedingly fragile, delicate, easily ripped. This is connected to my always repairing relationships, saying things to people to keep up appearances, maintain friendly relations; otherwise, life is back into incubation. My body says, I want you to leave me alone; leave me to my invisible incubator. [Ponteri]

*

By all accounts, we're programmed to be who and how we are, pretty much from birth.

The point is, You can't deny your own nature, even if your own nature is terribly flawed, even if it's ugly or annoying or hurtful to people, including yourself. [Robert Cohen]
Bummer.

Bummer, Janice Shapiro's first book, is about sadness, pain (especially self-punishment), and the drive to always locate satisfaction the next precinct over. This drive is often phrased as desire or sex or love or romance—the yearning for another—but to me all this sex talk is just a metaphor for the larger human hunger for "meaning," fulfillment, peace, which ain't gonna arrive, not in our lifetimes.

For if we could be satisfied in any way, we should have been satisfied long ago. [Seneca]

*

As a little kid, I would start every morning by promising myself (and inevitably failing to live up to the promise), Don't cry today.

I adopted a "Pity Me" face and then stared out of the passenger-side window so people in other cars could see that I was being abused. [Richard Smith]

Joan Acocella explains that the novelist Paula Fox, who was Courtney Love's grandmother, grew up with a very cold mother who had four abortions, didn't want Paula, and was inordinately neglectful. Acocella argues that when people grow up in an emotionally barren landscape, they tend to 1) become passive, 2) think of themselves as not being sure of their feelings and/or not sure they have feelings, and 3) if they're writers, get their revenge by not forgetting a thing and analyzing everyone, including themselves, in an unforgivably harsh light. Acocella writes about Fox, "The psychological consequence of hostility within a family is passivity. In her world, unloved children don't grow up to take heroin or kill somebody. They just develop a 'hardened heart,' a handicap that is as much perceptual as moral. Having denied the heart's feelings for so long, they no longer know what it feels."

My mother continually belittled me, mocked me, hit me, hated me, taught me to hate myself, and she's still a not insignificant part of my emotional landscape. Do I ever want to excise that?

*

A lifelong kink (not to be confused with some sexually adventurous experimentation) is just as hardwired into a person's sexuality as his sexual orientation. [Dan Savage]

And moreover my nature requires this; that's how I'm made. [Fyodor Dostoevsky]

—the tendency of passive infant males to be more dependent as adults on their wives or sweethearts than less passive infants. [Jerome Kagan]

Was I breast-fed?

Method of potty-training?

Did Mom ever forgive me for leaving out my toys, which caused her to trip down the stairs and badly break her arm (from which she never fully recovered)?

Deep into his eighties, I badgered my father with inane, embarrassing, microscopic questions such as these, seeking to find out how in the world I got wired this way (e.g., when I was learning to crawl and then walk, I'd cry and fuss, and when my mother picked me up, I'd cry and fuss even more). My mother had complete contempt for my father, blamed herself for marrying him, and despised me for reminding her of him (the first time I shaved, I cut myself all over, my father and I daubed the cuts with little pieces of toilet paper, which we thought looked funny and so showed my mother, who shrieked at my father and me for our incompetence). Ashkenazi Jews and masochism—that connection? (Milton Berle, declining a glass of wine at a Shriners event: "Jews don't drink; it interferes with our suffering.") Manic-depressive fathers and masochism—that connection? I'm grasping at straw dogs.

All of us are wounded, and the deepest wound always comes back to sex. [Tisdale]

Or: DNA, family, environment, innate temperament; difficult to divine, of course, what factor or combination of factors is instrumental.

Or: It's in the writer's interest to insure that the wound never heals. The animus it produces is too valuable. [Richard Stern]

How did I get wired this way?
I don't get it.
Do I want to get it?
Do I want to get over it?
(Do you want me to get over it?)

*

In the US, Jewish intermarriage has doubled during the last two decades, and current estimates suggest that it stands at [around 58] percent. The antipathy that exists between Jewish men and Jewish women is cited as a significant factor in that rate. [Estelle Frankel]

His eyes were similar to mine, to Les's, and to Boo Boo's, in that the eyes of this bunch could all be rather bashfully described as extra-dark oxtail in color or Plaintive Jewish Brown. [Salinger]

What once was rabbinic hyperbole, however, now understates the problem. In my work as a counselor, I hear Jewish men complain that Jewish women make them feel less manly. By the same token, Jewish women assert that their femininity is not as appreciated by Jewish men as it is by non-Jewish men. Behind these gripes lies more than the standard war between the sexes. For when it comes to mating practices between Jewish men and Jewish women today, the struggle is compounded by a hornet's nest of psychohistorical and cultural factors. [Frankel]

—Jewish self-hatred as the cause of so many Jewish men and Jewish women "intermarrying."

Obviously, it's not a coincidence that you're not Jewish, whereas almost all of my girlfriends were.

*

I was very sexual as a child. At first, it had nothing to do with indifference or power. It was purely libidinal. When I was about 3, I rode (naked and completely aroused) on the shoulders of a neighbor boy. I remember my genitals throbbing. [Phillips]

"Talent. I don't have *talent*. I have willingness. What *talent*?" As a kid, she had always told the raunchiest jokes. As an adult, she could rip open a bone and speak out of it. Simple, clear. There was never anything to stop her. Why was there never anything to stop her? "I can stretch out the neck of a sweater to point at a freckle on my shoulder. Anyone who didn't get enough attention in nursery school can do that. Talent is something else." [Lorrie Moore]

People will say about an especially pretty little girl, "She's gonna be a heartbreaker"—which is, to me, an odd and revealing phrase. What does it mean, exactly? It means that when she grows up, she will use her beauty as a weapon (and is expected to).

—the hauteur of the female child who knows it won't be long before she is nubile and has the power to hurt. [Bellow]

Our (then) twelve-year-old daughter, to me:
You're not the boss of me.

When our daughter was fourteen, she asked me why some people wear clothes that say OBEY.

Reader, I knew.

Why do I find an upsweep (even the word "upsweep") so sexy?

The pinning, the entrapment, the promised/refused cascade, the regal self-swaddling.

But it's Ms. Fanning, with the cruel eyes and sleekly upswept hair suggestive of an underage dominatrix, who shows real bite. Mr. Weitz doesn't know what to do with her, but when she smiles, you finally see the darker side of desire. [Manohla Dargis]

Looking back at losing my virginity, I wish I had turned off Aerosmith. . . . Losing my virginity was a nightmare I wouldn't wish on Hitler. [options in the *Stranger*'s 5th Annual Sex Survey]

—dressed to kill.

—the incredibly powerful psycho-sexual-socio-economic subtext underlying the idea that someone (me) "outkicked his coverage": married someone far more attractive (you).

*

I've never had the courage to want the world. I've always let it come to me, which of course is a rather passive approach to existence, but the funny thing is: inevitably, it comes. Sooner or later, whether I wanted it or not, the world came to me; it came at me, it keeps coming at me.

I was a strong-willed child with a lot of aggressive impulses, which, for various reasons, I was actively discouraged from developing. They stayed hidden under a surface of extreme passivity, and when they did appear it was often in a wildly irresponsible, almost crazy way. [Mary Gaitskill]

I thought _____ was trying to teach me how to live, which she was, and I didn't like that. I wanted to remember and remain who I'd always been: a nervous little boy cowering in the corner.

When he was a little boy, Dave used to sit, rapt, in front of the TV during *Batman* and old westerns because women were often tied up, left squirming and in peril. There was something exciting about the idea that he could rescue the damsel in distress. On the other hand, there was also something exciting about imagining himself the villain who put her there in the first place. [Brian Alexander]

My father was very sick. I knew he was going to die. I learned as a very young person to close off, to not be hurt. So I distanced myself. Unfortunately, when you're ten years old, you can't distance yourself from one thing without distancing yourself from everything. I was just emotionally disconnected. And, that night in Boston, I plugged in. I reconnected. But, to this day, I have remnants of it. [Albert Brooks]

Do you think it's possible that I've enlisted you to cure my heart by killing it?

*

Whatever my older sister had, I, by definition, wanted, because it had attained this one quality: it was outside my consciousness. The moment I held it, my mind experienced it, so I no longer wanted it. All week long, my sister and I would think and talk about *Batman* or *Get Smart* or *The Addams Family*— whatever the show was that year—and on the night of the show we'd make sugar cookies and root beer floats, then set up TV trays; immediately after the show, we'd talk about how much we hated that it was over and what agony it was going to be to wait an entire week for it to be on again, whereas the episode itself was usually only so-so, hard to remember, over before you knew it.

In my late twenties, I admired the Boy Scout belt a friend of mine was wearing—I liked the way it was a joke about uniformity (OBEY) at the same time it simply looked good—and when I asked where he got it, he said, to my astonishment, that it was his original Boy Scout belt: he still had it; he could still wear it; he was skinny, stylish, striking. I never made it past the Cub Scouts and even in the Cubs failed to distinguish myself (shiny shoes and slip knots have never been very high priorities for me). Still, I wanted a Boy Scout belt and thought it would be easy. I stopped in at a BSA office, where I was told that clothing and accessories could be purchased only by Scouts or troop leaders. I went so far as to schedule an interview for a troop leader position until, fearing accusations of pedophilia, I ended the charade. Visits to several stores led me to the boys' department of JC Penney, which carried Boy Scout uniforms in their catalogue and told me I could order a belt. I wore it once, maybe twice, with jeans, then tossed it into the back of the closet.

An object in possession seldom retains the same charm that it had in pursuit. [Pliny the Elder]
In ancient Greek language and culture, "eros" has very little to do with love; it has to do with absence.
Desire is a relation of being to lack. [Jacques Lacan]
The true paradises are paradises we have lost. [Marcel Proust]
Like a face crossing a mirror at the back of the room, Eros moves. You reach. Eros is gone. [Anne Carson]
Eros is a bastard got by Wealth on Poverty and ever at home in a life of want. [Plato]

It's endless, in other words—this not getting what we want:

I loved Don Adams as Maxwell Smart. I loved Edward Platt as the Chief (Daddy = failure). I loved the cone of silence as it descended upon Max and the Chief, because even at age seven, I knew it was a metaphor for human miscommunication. But it was Barbara Feldon I was in love with: Agent 99 (as close as they could get to calling her Agent 69 without calling her that). The purr in her voice, the way she towered over Max, and yet the way he was oblivious to her worship (which was the mirror, of course, of our genuflection to her; she pretended to be oblivious to how much we worshipped her) . . . her alternate coaxing and chiding of Agent 86 (his number meant he was binnable) . . . Max as dumb/smart (his stupidity was his gallantry; he got that life is a joke) . . . all the au courant Courrèges and Paco Rabanne outfits she wore, the Vidal Sassoon cut . . . . Either *Get Smart* mapped my entire sexual life over the next fifty years or my psyche got back-formed onto the show. All the comedy is on one side—all the Jewishness (Don Adams was raised Catholic, his mother's faith, while his brother was raised Jewish, his father's faith, which is too perfect); Feldon as deadpan WASP, as sex goddess, ice queen as savior, as very subtle (quasi-unaware) sadist. . . . The show killed me, still kills me ("missed it by that much").

*

My sister and I were just kids in 1965—ten and nine, respectively—when my parents hired a guy named Gil to paint the inside of our house; after Gil left, my mother discovered the word FUCK etched into the new white paint in the dining room. I'd never seen my mother so infuriated. Had my parents underpaid or somehow mistreated Gil, and had this been his low revenge? He adamantly denied it, offering to return to rectify the problem. Had my sister or I done it?

We insisted we hadn't, and I'm confident we were telling the truth. I, in any case was (I think); I can't speak for my usually well-behaved sister. Although over time the inscription lost its hold on my mother's imagination, FUCK remained—if faintly—and continued to cast a subtle, mysterious spell over the dining room for the remainder of my childhood.

When discussing dollar amounts of a nearly consummated deal, literary agents—nearly without exception, I've found—suddenly start cursing at a far higher rate than usual.

In high school, the colonizing nature of my own gaze overwhelmed me: I couldn't keep looking at a girl once she'd seen me looking at her, i.e., looked back. This wasn't a lot of help to me on the dating scene. Saturday nights were exhausting: first Sally Struthers, then Mary Tyler Moore, then Suzanne Pleshette—all on CBS.

I was nineteen years old and a virgin, and at first I read Rebecca's journal because I needed to know what to do next and what she liked to hear. Every little gesture, every minor movement I made she passionately described and whole-heartedly admired. When we were kissing or swimming or walking down the street, I could hardly wait to rush back to her room to find out what phrase or what twist of my body had been lauded in her journal. I loved her impatient hand-writing, her purple ink, the melodrama of the whole thing. It was such a surprising and addictive respite, seeing every aspect of my being celebrated by someone else rather than excoriated by myself. She wrote, "I've never truly loved any-one the way I love D and it's never been so total and com-plete, yet so unpossessing and pure, and sometimes I want to drink him in like golden water." I found it difficult to concen-trate on my Wordsworth midterm after reading that about myself. . . . Weeks passed; guilt grew. I told Rebecca that I'd read her journal. Why couldn't I just live with the knowledge

and let the shame dissipate over time? What was—what is—
the matter with me? Do I just have a bigger self-destruct but-
ton (and like to push it harder and more incessantly) than
everyone else? Of course. But also the language of the events
was at least as erotic to me as the events themselves, and when
I was no longer reading her words, I was no longer very adamantly in love with Rebecca.

This is what is known as a tragic flaw.

*

My father's first marriage ended when he had his affair with a
gorgeous, red-haired editor at the *Los Angeles Herald-Express*;
a picture of her appeared—somewhat bizarrely—in our family photo album.

Our fifth-grade social studies teacher had supposedly
once been Playmate of the Month. This rumor could never
be confirmed or denied, but for the first and last time in my
life I got a C. No one in that class—boys or girls—could concentrate on anything except Miss Acker.

"Petite Nancy Spiess, a Detroit Bunny and a motorcycle
buff," was the first figure in a magazine to whom I ever masturbated. Those silver fingernails, that green bikini bottom—
I couldn't stop imagining her in the buff, on the back of a
motorcycle.

—one of the relatively few traits of my own that I like: I
find other people interesting.

Trained by my journalist-parents, I know how to drag out
of people their most damaging secrets—to lord them (the
secrets) over them (the people).

I don't like that part as much.

I read in the *San Francisco Chronicle* that the stripper Carol Doda was "statuesque." I didn't know what the word meant—I was eleven—but in one important feature my babysitter resembled Carol Doda, so I asked her whether she was statuesque. She said she didn't know what that meant, but we could look it up.

When she noticed me going first thing all the time now to "Daily Punch," the *San Francisco Chronicle's* art section, my mother praised me for finally taking a lively interest in cultural affairs. I especially liked the Question Man, from whom I won ten or twenty-five dollars at age twelve for submitting the question "How do you impress a woman?" It was a legitimate concern of mine in the sixth grade, what with my mother seeming to be pretty much unwinnable, and I remember going to school the day the Question Man used my question and feeling intuitively that the way to impress women was to appear oblivious to them while performing an arduous feat intently and well, so I slid down the banister on my hip. I'm not sure I'd answer the question very differently even now.

By the spring of 1971, the Question Man was losing his allure for me, the theatre reviews and editorial cartoons had misplaced their pungency, and movies about sadomasochism alone retained my interest. Or, more precisely, advertisements for movies about sadomasochism (the back page of "Daily Punch" was solid every morning with commercials for onanism), since I had yet to see one, and less the blurry images in the ads than the words, whose inevitable alliteration ("Debasement, debauchery, and defilement—beyond human dignity!") sounded like the tintinnabulation of desire.

I was particularly partial to the ink screens covering certain words and certain body parts in ads for films. It's the most transparent ruse, but I found it always worked.

Why?

Because it glamorizes the unavailable.

*

When I was in sixth grade, a guy said he wanted to kiss me. I said, "You can't kiss my face until you kiss my feet." I took off my shoe—I had a sandal on—and he said, "No, you're kidding." I was pretty limber, and I put my foot up on his shoulder and said, "Come on, seriously," so he said, "Okay [lifts her left foot and points it delicately at me]." That first time, I don't know what I knew. I just knew that I wanted to make him kiss my foot before he ever got the honor to kiss me. He kissed my foot a whole bunch, then got into it really well and kissed my leg. I said, "Let's go over to the park," and we just started petting. From then on, he did what I said, like going down on me. ["Tammy," Q&A with Robert Stoller]

Samuel Johnson had scars all over his face, he twitched, every time he walked past a picket fence he had to touch every picket in the fence, and out of his mouth came amazing things. As Gopnik explains, Johnson addressed Hester Thrale as "Mistress," begged her to "spare me the need to constrain myself, by taking away the power to leave the room when you want me to stay," and asked her to "keep me in that form of slavery which you know so well how to make blissful." She wrote back, "You were saying on Sunday that of all the unhappy you were the happiest, in consequence of my Attention to your Complaint." In *Anecdotes of the Late Samuel Johnson,* she could hardly be more explicit, "Says Johnson a Woman has *such* power between the Ages of twenty five and forty five, that She may tye a Man to a post and whip him if She will. This he knew of him self was literally and strictly true."

—my obsession as a kid with this (surely apocryphal?) story:
A prisoner of war is stripped naked and placed just an inch or so from an electrified fence that will kill him if it touches

him. A gorgeous woman dances naked all around him, daring him to respond. If he responds, he's dead.

I'm riveted when people are forced to yield to the demands of war: the moment in *Hearts and Minds* when two US soldiers, fondling their Vietnamese prostitutes, survey the centerfolds taped to the mirrored walls and (for the benefit of the camera) try to imitate heroic masculinity.

—Jack Nicholson's view that it's all-out war between men and women, that women are much smarter and tougher than men; also, Nicholson's devotion to spanking (at age thirty-seven, he found out that the woman he thought was his sister was in fact his mother—the basis, of course, of that *Chinatown* subplot); so, too, his preference to sleep alone, his (to you, admirable) acceptance of the divide.

For a while in my last marriage my husband didn't want to have sex with me, so I pretended I wasn't interested in having sex with him. This, predictably, revitalized his interest in me and so for a while we each got what we wanted. But I had to keep pretending that I wasn't interested and at a certain point I really wasn't interested (I turned into what I was pretending to be), so the prevailing story of our marriage is that I never wanted to have sex. . . . Does being in charge always involve indifference? Vice versa? Can one jockey for dominance in a relationship by feigning indifference? [Phillips]

Female indifference has always been incredibly erotic to me.

*

Obama: Someone once said that every man is trying to either live up to his father's expectations or make up for his father's mistakes, and I suppose that may explain my particular malady as well as anything else.

Obama is, obviously, the latter (although, predictably, he pretends to be both).

So am I (the latter).

My mother would often say to me, If you keep going in this direction, you're going to wind up like your father.

My shrink could barely believe she said this once, let alone dozens of times.

Same shrink (too easy, but still): Emotionally, your mother raped you all.

When people speak of maternal nourishment or paternal authority, I literally have no idea what they're talking about.

My mother was a terrifying figure of Olympian hauteur and disdain; my father was a severe manic-depressive and ECT devotee who was in and out of mental hospitals his entire adult life.

His role wasn't to be a caretaker; it was to be cared for (my mother called this the "tyranny of the weak").

He occasionally liked to say, in his sharp Brooklyn accent, virtually under his breath, to my mother, Shaddup.

Once, early in their marriage, he apparently shoved her; my mother never stopped alluding to this moment when, very briefly, their roles got reversed.

*

Get the fuck out of here, you fucking bitch. What the fuck do I care?
—something I once actually said, thirty years ago, attempting to break up with you when you said my father had never taught me how to be a man (he hadn't).

Like dialogue in a snuff film.

Like a parody of misogyny.

Cliché of clichés; fact of facts: it made me feel male/got me hard, saying what I said.

Is there any writer I love—from Epictetus to Simon Gray—whose work doesn't specialize in self-demolition?

(Was there, by the way, any "major" modernist writer—Kafka, Woolf, Proust, Mann, Joyce, Eliot—who wasn't flagrantly masochistic?)

One of my favorite books ever is Gray's four-volume *Smoking Diaries,* in which his alter ego is the self-serious and bombastic Harold Pinter.

It's painful, though, to watch interviews with both men.

Pinter is (come what will) a man.

Gray is a victim, an infant.

*

I married someone who was, I thought, the complete opposite of my mother and turned her—turned you—into her, the question being, of course, whether you intuited that and became that way on purpose to satisfy what you knew was my deepest drive, or whether I knew (and you knew) all along you had that reservoir of coldness.

—Freud's notion that there are always at least four people in every bedroom, the key questions being, Who are they? Where are they? Where are they hiding? In whom? In college, reading all those Greek tragedies and listening to the lectures about them, I would think, rather blithely, Well, that tragic flaw thing is nicely symmetrical; whatever makes Oedipus heroic is also—What did I know then? Nothing. I didn't feel in my bones as I do now that what powers our drive assures our downfall, that our birth date is our death sentence. The king was fated to kill his dad and marry his mom, so they sent him away. He lived with his new mom and dad, found out about the curse, ran off and killed his real dad, married his real mom. It was a set-up. He had to test it. Even though he knew it would cost him his eyes, he had to do it. He had to push ahead. He had to prove who he was.

Upon my return, after I'd been gone quite a while, you said, *Fuck me, you pig.* You'd never said anything remotely like this to me before. I think we're all always saying, "Fuck me, you pig," to people who aren't the pigs we want to be fucked by, no? Or, hey, maybe I was indeed that pig. One never knows, does one?

"If you can't be with the one you love," my friend says, "love the one who looks like the one you love." Other people call this having a type. It's an expression of grief for an original loss. [Sarah Manguso]

According to Maureen Paton, "A subtly revealing scene from the first screen drama about the relationship [between Philip Larkin and Monica Jones] suggests that the commitment-phobic Larkin was more interested in spanking than actual sex." Larkin had acknowledged, "I have built Monica in my image. I've made her dependent on me and now I can't abandon her." The film's director, Susanna White, said, "We wanted to show the emotional complexity of it all, the man (dominated by his mother) who didn't want to commit to marriage for serious, complicated reasons; he thought he was better off on his own. And we wanted to show the human cost of that, which I hope is what people are going to carry away from it. It isn't just another bit of sex on BBC2."

My mother reviled me.
I can feel that in every footfall.
My half-brother's mother adored him, which has made him fat and sassy and self-satisfied and happy.
Poor bastard.

According to my astrologer-friend, Cancers who have never had mother love are doomed.
I love that.
I love the tragedy of that.

*

I carried a Swiss Army knife with me, a nice one that my father had bought for me in one of the shops in Al Khabar, and one night it occurred to me that I should see how many times I could cut the skin on my forearm until I lost my nerve. Then I did my stomach, my shins. I came back to the dorm room with the sleeves and front of my flannel shirt sticking to me in tiny, stinging places, but I felt as if I'd actually been somewhere, as if for the first time in a long time I knew exactly where on the globe I was—one specific point now, alone, not me as part of a family, or me playing in the creek with my brother—and the discovery was both loneliness-making and invigorating. [Rachel Starnes]

Were you a cutter?

I was an angsty teenager. I'm not allowed to cut myself anymore. Now I have somebody else do it. ["Keda," Q&A with Alexander]

Eventually, as a hobby, I began to scratch my arms hard enough to leave red marks even when they didn't itch. [Hunt]

Renata Adler. Anne Carson. Terry Castle. Emily Dickinson. Joan Didion. Manohla Dargis. Marguerite Duras. Annie Ernaux. Pauline Kael. Laura Kipnis. Violette Leduc. Rosemary Mahoney. Janet Malcolm. Sylvia Plath. Sappho. Et alia. My obsession with women writers whose words are etched in acid.

*

I knew a guy in high school—the best point guard I've ever played against—who lit kittens on fire and threw them off the roof of the twenty-three-floor apartment building in which he lived with his older sister. I often wonder what if anything he's doing now. (Internet searches turn up next to nothing.)

I can never stop thinking about the afternoon when, at age fifteen, I was playing basketball by myself; two girls and a boy asked if I wanted to go make out with the girl who didn't have a boyfriend, and I said, No thanks—I need to work on my turnaround jumper.

I tried to show off for you during a pick-up basketball game by taking and making shot after shot after shot from the top of the key; your only response was, *You should pass more.*

Interviewing Phil Jackson twenty years ago, I was startled by how comfortable he was with being plainly unlikeable—with what Kobe Bryant once called, in another context, "the ugliness of greatness."

—my switching madly back and forth between National Public Repetition and sports radio; the dark-haired male anchor paired inevitably with the blonde female anchor; black athletes and their obsession with Kim Kardashian types . . .

What would it do to someone to be worshipped wherever she goes?

What would it be like to be J. R. Smith and ask a Twitter follower, in all seriousness, You trying to get the pipe?

I used to be a basketball fan, but I was never a fan of the dunk; dominion bores me.

I once felt joy in being alive and I felt this mainly when I was playing basketball and I rarely if ever feel that joy anymore and it's my own damn fault and that's life. Too bad.

*

My college roommate, to me: I can't stand cats; they're like women.

Dogs: self-parody of devotional loyalty; cats: self-parody of irremediable narcissism.

—the instinctive connection I feel with nearly all dogs; the natural antipathy between almost all cats and me.

She pats your head and says, Good boy, that's a good boy, although you're not sure whether she's saying good boy or good dog. You feel a little excited about that. The dog part. Don't be embarrassed. I know these things. It's my job. [Jamie Callan]

—the truly maniacal attention you lavished on our cat, the only being toward whom I've ever seen you express unalloyed care, affection, devotion, and love.

If I had to say why I didn't always entirely embrace that furry, purring creature, I suppose it's because it was always scratching at me for something or stretched out on all fours for me to scratch it, like human desire reduced to the lowest common denominator.

Do you like animals?
I prefer people.
Animals have a heart, too.
Maybe, but I prefer people.
I don't always.
. . .
I wonder which is the cutest kitty.
I want the kitty no one else wants.

*

As a child, Richard Berendzen was stricken with rheumatic fever, which confined him to his bed for nearly three years. During that time the youngster would gaze at the stars, he once recalled, and wonder, "Does space end? Did it begin? Has it always existed?" In the past year, Berendzen developed a certain paranoia about his personal safety, even ordering one-way glass for his office windows. Then on April 8, Berendzen abruptly stepped down as president of American University, citing "exhaustion." Two weeks later the real reason for his resignation burst over the Northwest Washington campus like a supernova: authorities in Fairfax County, Virginia, disclosed that Berendzen, who is married and the father of two grown children, was believed responsible for making dozens of obscene telephone calls from his university office. [Bill Hewitt and Garry Clifford]

Sterry had clients who seemed to be reenacting a past sexual trauma. One woman in particular would lie in bed and have him silently crawl under the covers and "orally pleasure her while she lay there like she was dead." He says, "I knew someone did something to her, you know? Every single time she wanted exactly the same thing." [Tracy Clark-Flory]

Bobby Knight's aberrant behavior (throwing chairs, abusing players, being photographed raising a bullwhip over a black player) was secondary to the humiliation the behavior brought him. The "transgression" offered "pleasure," but it was principally an avenue by which to return to a familiar landscape of disgrace and shame, otherwise known as childhood. (C'est moi.)

*

Erotic fantasy is full of violence and disguise. It's a theatre of the mind whose props are the negated impulses of childhood. [Julia O'Faolain]

In this view, the scenario of a perverse fantasy is a disguised repetition of a childhood emotional trauma. But because the fantasy brings sexual pleasure, the perversion becomes a way to turn childhood trauma into a triumph of sorts. Perversions typically originate in reaction to painful emotional feelings. [Daniel Goleman]

Sexual perversion is a way of mastering earlier emotional trauma through scenarios that add sexual pleasures to the wound. [Wayne Myers]

The more severe the suffering in childhood, the greater the need for SM; the more the suffering was physical, the more physical suffering will be manifest in the perversion. [Stoller]

The erotic pleasure in a perverse act is secondary to the emotional reassurance it offers. [Louise Kaplan]

Love is governed by unconscious forces causing us to attach ourselves to somebody with whom we can repeat a self-harming pleasure. [Goleman]

Sexuality is lawless or it is nothing, not least because of its rootedness in our unconscious lives, where all sexual certainties come to grief. [Jacqueline Rose]

Love is giving something you don't have to someone who doesn't want it. [Lacan]

When a child of any age shows intentional cruelty toward animals that is repeated, severe, and without remorse, this should be taken very seriously. It's crucial to keep animals safe, but also childhood animal abuse is linked to other forms of violence and psychopathology. A child who abuses animals requires immediate intervention and treatment. Animal abuse is often the first manifestation of serious emotional turmoil that may escalate into extreme violence, such as mass killing. Jeffrey Dahmer, Albert DeSalvo (the "Boston Strangler"), David Berkowitz (the "Son of Sam") and Carroll Edward Cole, a serial killer accused of thirty-five deaths, all recounted animal torture as their first violent act. [Gail Melson]

The two other key predictors of sadism in adulthood are bed-wetting and fire-starting.

What probably matters most is what sexual serial killers think about when they masturbate—the intentional pairing of certain imagery with sexual pleasure. On the screen, the babysitter starts to take off her bra, which makes the kid in the audience get sexually excited. Then Jason comes in and decapitates her. [Park Dietz]

In the brain, the pathways that regulate sexual, aggressive, and predatory impulses are very close together. [John Money]

Without exception, all sociopaths show reduced activity in the prefrontal cortex (seat of judgment, planning, and thoughtfulness), overactivity in the anterior cingulate gyrus (the brain's gearshift, which allows it to segue from one thought to another), and abnormalities in the left temporal lobe (involved in mood and temper control). [Sharon Begley]

If someone has a left-temporal-lobe problem, he has dark, awful, violent thoughts. If he has a cingulate-gyrus problem as well, he gets stuck on the bad thoughts. And if he has a prefrontal-cortex problem, he can't supervise the bad thoughts he gets stuck on. [Daniel Amen]

Abuse seems to leave a physical trace on the developing brain, assaulting it with a constant barrage of stress hormones. The result is that the child becomes inured to stress and, indeed, to most feeling. Emotionally, he flatlines. He can no longer perceive another human being's distress; he can't feel what someone else is feeling. One of the most consistent findings about the biology of violence is that sadists and cold-blooded killers show virtually no response to stress—no racing heart, no sweating, no adrenaline rush. [Begley]

Shields's novel-in-stories, *Handbook for Drowning*, painfully, accurately chronicles the endemic disease of our time: the difficulty of feeling. [Rhoda Koenig]

*

A group of us six- and seven- and eight-year-old kids would all gather in someone's playroom and be called, one by one, into the dimmer and grimier laundry area, where we were positioned face up on a table under a bare light bulb—to be probed by a group of powerful girls, who would reach beneath our clothing and feel around while asking us very stern questions.

Sex is a Nazi. The students all knew
this at your school. [Les Murray]

In high school, I was athletic and thus, to a certain extent, popular. However, I worked unduly hard at it, at sports, with very little sprezzatura, which made me extremely unpopular among the dozen or so really popular, athletic people. Why? Because I made popularity or grace look like something less than a pure gift. Only the dozen or so really popular, athletic people knew I was unpopular, so I could, for instance, be elected, if I remember correctly (I don't; I'm making this up), vice-president of the junior class and yet be, in a sense, underappreciated. It was a frustrating place to reign, really, consigned to the highest ring of the Ringstrasse, unable to escape or improve. Every Halloween I cowered in my basement bedroom with the doors locked, lights out, shades down, and listened to the sound of lobbed eggs.

In the fall of 1972, I broke my leg, badly, playing football on the beach (so Kennedyesque!), and the first day I was home from the hospital I lay immobile in a body cast in the living room, an aluminum pin in my thigh. Two medics carrying a stretcher stormed the front door, looking for someone who had supposedly fallen on the front steps. Later that afternoon, a middle-aged man, wearing a Giants windbreaker, tried to deliver a pepperoni pizza. A dump truck started pouring a ton of gravel into our miniscule backyard. A cop came to investigate a purported robbery. Another ambulance. A florist. An undertaker from central casting. A paint salesman. My popular, athletic friends, who had gathered together to watch the proceedings with binoculars in one of their houses at the top of the hill, orchestrated this traffic all night and deep into the morning.

They meant it as a terrorizing, thoroughly evil prank, and my mother certainly saw it that way (they called me "Buddha Boy"—the only Jewish kid among this group of jocks), but I never took it as anything other than the most moving, collective confession of the pain that consists of the inability to identify with someone else's pain other than by intensifying it. Vehicles from most areas of the service sector were parked, at one point, virtually around the block.

*

An extraordinary pall fell over the dining room table when, senior year of high school (my sister was away at college; I was trapped at dinner each night with my miserably married parents), trying to come up with rhymes for the words "pig" and "sick," I landed on "big" and "dick."

The single woman across the street has an English Mastiff named Maximus, with whom she parades around the neighborhood proudly. Am I the only person who thinks she's advertising that she's a size queen?

A study from Meston's lab showed a strong correlation between how erect a man's penis is and how aroused he says he is. [Elizabeth Landau]

Joke told to me by Brenda:
Why are girls so bad at math?
[holding index finger two inches from thumb] Because men keep telling them this is eight inches.

I think women say size isn't important, but when they talk to each other, they acknowledge that it's more important than they let on to men. It's one of the lies women tell. [Megan Griswold]

A woman who was attempting to seduce me and who apparently has small breasts informed me that "anything more than a handful is a waste."

—my sense that the kids in the swimming pool locker room are sniggering at my small penis; I want to explain to them that, reportedly like Jude Law, I'm a "grow-er" (six-plus inches!), not a "show-er."

*

Human intercourse is often one person's obstinate attempt to dominate another person, and an unfortunate fact about disfluency is that I've never been able to dominate. It's all very well and good to assert that communication comes down to a mad dogfight, but it's something else altogether to confess that I'm always the poor pup who loses. Another unfortunate fact about disfluency is that it's prevented me from ever entirely losing self-consciousness when expressing such traditional and truly important emotions as love, hate, joy, and deep pain. Always first aware not of the naked feeling itself but of the best way to phrase the feeling so as to avoid verbal repetition, I've come to think of emotions as belonging to other people, being the world's happy property but not mine—not really mine except by way of disingenuous circumlocution. As a child (when the stutter was at its worst), I could feel precisely where in my mouth language could communicate only language itself.

I have oversensitive antennae tuned to human miscommunication, misconnection, slight slights expressed via tone, love at first slight.

If one person makes you defensive, then that person is probably bad for you; if nearly everyone does, then you're probably bad for you. The answer, if you need more of an answer: you can be "bad for you" in two general ways—by seeking out relationships with highly critical people or by taking even the most harmless remarks as criticism. Or both, I suppose, if you like your maintenance high and your relationships testy. [Carolyn Hax]

—self-consciousness so extreme it almost precludes the minimal abandon necessary for the sexual act itself. [Katie Roiphe]

All stuttering is about is time: the (perceived) pressure to perform in the presence of a ticking clock.

The novelist John Hawkes said, about the first semi-decent thing I ever wrote (my sophomore year of college), that its true subject was the agony of love without communication and in the context of violence.

When we think of intimacy, we tend to think of love and its physical correspondent, sexual satisfaction. Intimacy in Ai's work is achieved not through sex but through violence. [Leslie McGrath]

Stuttering is not as much an issue for me now as it was in my teens and twenties; still, it's why I need sex to be so intimate, why I care so much about sex, especially oral sex.

—69 with me beneath you.

When I'm happy, I consume sweets to celebrate. When I'm upset, I eat treats as consolation. I'm therefore rarely without a reason to be in the throes of sugar shock. I don't drink. I don't smoke. I don't do drugs. I do candy, in massive doses. So what? Who doesn't? What's the harm? Much of the glory of glucose overload is the way it mimics the biochemical frenzy of a full-blown speech block and crystallizes it into the pure adrenaline of a brief, happy high (followed quickly by a crash). To me, sugar consumption is a gorgeous allegory about intractable reality and very temporary transcendence.

In Amy Hempel's "In the Animal Shelter," the beautiful, abandoned women reject the abandoned animals in order to reverse the rejection but also to re-experience the rejection.

—ceaseless articulation as attempt at revenge upon (but also, clearly, a revisitation of) stuttering.

*

I kissed nearly no one until I was seventeen (horrific acne throughout adolescence).

The record repeated, over and over, the assertion that if he couldn't love her, he didn't want to love nobody.

In late adolescence, I worried that there would always be a glass wall between myself and the world and wondered if this was a phenomenon unique to myself; I thought probably not. Still, I had doubts.

According to Leonard Michaels, Real intimacy is for the world, not a friend.

Our daughter's friend is in a bike accident.
My sympathy slides into invasive investigation.
Don't become—don't be—that creepy older guy who asks teenage girls too many questions about their lives.

*

You're forty, you said to me twenty years ago. *Time to move on and let our daughter be the needy one.*
You still don't understand why teenagers put metal hoops in their faces.

Hawkes would often solemnly inform me, I am obsessed with sex and death.
I would mock him, though only to myself, thinking, What is there to say about these two things other than that sex is good and death is bad?
I was nineteen, twenty, twenty-one, knew exactly nothing.

Everything I learned in graduate school came the first semester of the first year, when the old-goat teacher handed to my gorgeous, brilliant, lazy classmate a bouquet of flowers (to express his appreciation of what he imagined to be the gorgeousness of her vagina), which she immediately "garbaged"—her word.

Hawkes makes terror rather than love the center of his work, knowing all the while, of course, that there can be no terror without the hope for love and love's defeat. It is not so much the fact that love succumbs to terror which obsesses Hawkes as the fact that love breeding terror is itself the final terror. [Leslie Fiedler]

Who wants to watch romance? I'd rather watch scary.

Why do all your favorite books about marriage include a dead spouse?

I sometimes think I've spent the last forty years of my life trying to make my dead mother not hate me (hate me more?).

*

I became imbued with the notion that to carry dirt from one spot to another was to spread germs and endanger people's lives. In the house, this was easy enough to avoid. If I remembered to leave my shoes on the back porch, then showered six or seven times and washed my hands every time I came in contact with something, I was in little to no danger of distributing any mud. Outdoors, especially, on the playground, though, I'd be running merrily across the yard, step in a puddle, realized what I'd done, then run back and soak until I felt the dirt had returned to its point of origin. I used to spend entire recesses digging my heel into a grease spot I suspected of being the repository of the black spot on my white high-top Converse.

—anilingus as a recurrent fantasy, corporealizing as it does my frequent feeling that, as a stutterer, I have a mouth full of shit.

When we have drunk sex, my boyfriend always wants to lick my asshole while going down on me. It always grosses me out, so I stop him, just 'cause I don't think it's sanitary. It feels good, though, and I wouldn't mind him doing it. I'm just worried about the cleanliness of it. Is there anything I can do before I go out, when I shower, anything like that? [comment on Reddit]

Girls with asses like mine do not talk to boys with faces like yours. [Karen McCullah Lutz]

—the sex-bomb standing in line next to me and asking, Whose ass do you think you have to kiss to get in?

What makes Pippa Middleton's ass so sexy? It seems to be talking to me. It's saying, Kiss my ass.

—your obvious embarrassment, when we were playing a game of Pictionary with another couple, over the fact that I knew what "callipygian" means.

He would do anything for me, even eat my shit. We don't do that, but we talk about it—that he would. That excites me. He pushes himself into my underwear, pushes his nose into my bottom. We like it that he climbs up under my dress, that what he's doing is wrong. And he's covered by my long clothes. He's under here, but no one can necessarily see him. He degrades himself to do that for me, okay? ["Tammy," Q&A with Stoller]

Have you ever made love for six hours, barely stopping? Have you ever had nine orgasms in a night? Have you ever seen me weep from the sight of your beauty? When was the last time we slept in each other's arms? Have you ever seen my savage side? Have you ever known me to be absolutely helpless with passion? Has anyone ever stuck their tongue up your ass? Have you risked disgrace for me? Have you made a double life and been willing to hurt another person for the love of me? [Spencer]

I need a man who will worship and slap my ass, pull my hair, choke me, call me a sexy bitch, kiss me like he loves me, and fuck me like he hates me. [porn chat room]

That's enough ass-licking, slave. Now I want you to eat my asshole. And lick it deep enough to taste my shit. [porn chat room]

When I'm driving, looking out the window and noticing a woman with a great ass, as I strain to see her face, how does she know to keep turning so the back of her head is always toward me?
Wow, that guy must have a really high sperm count to flash his lights like that.
—the inescapable conclusion that the shape of a high-end sports car's rear end is meant to replicate a bubble-butted woman's.

Thanks, but no—one asshole in my pants is enough. [line of dialogue in student's essay]

How do you account for the truly incredible emphasis, not just in your movies but in the industry in general, on anal sex?
Assholes are reality. Pussies are bullshit. [John Stagliano, Q&A with Martin Amis]

I know a man who attempted to grapple in analysis with the question of why he was attracted only to blonde women. "I suppose," he said to the analyst, "that it's because angels are blonde, as are princesses in fairy tales. Blondes are golden; they belong to the dominant ethnic type." The analyst said, "That has nothing to do with it. You're attracted to blondes for quite a simple reason: they are furthest from the color of feces." [Anatole Broyard]

—Alfred Hitchcock (whose mother would force him to stand at the foot of his bed for several hours as punishment) and cold, regal blondes.

One social researcher at UCLA has been studying the trend of "anal bleaching," the use of lighteners to reduce the contrast between the anus and surrounding skin, so anal sex enthusiasts have pretty rectums. [Alexander]

Barbra Streisand chooses her projects very carefully; it has been three years since her show-offy star turn as a nut in *Nuts*, and only now has she rededicated herself to film, this time as the producer-director-star-despot of *The Prince of Tides*, an adaptation of Pat Conroy's novel that her ex-boyfriend Jon Peters is paying her to make for Columbia Pictures. Streisand's on-the-set demeanor suggests that the *Nuts* magic has yet to wear off: not too long ago, she chewed out her staff because her trailer was inappropriately equipped. The problem? The motor home's toilet featured an awkwardly placed flush handle that in the cramped trailer required its user to pivot around and risk experiencing a glimpse into the bowl. Under Streisand's maniacal orders, plans were drawn up, at considerable expense, to remount the flushing mechanism so that she would be spared the apparent trauma of turning around. Alas, even this proposed solution failed to satisfy Streisand, who as producer of the film is nominally responsible for keeping the film within budget. She finally decreed that henceforth her underlings find and rent her *houses* near various shooting locations—the main criterion being the grandeur of the houses' bathrooms. [Jamie Malanowski]

Question to my friend Nancy Williams via email: In Rome, I was struck by how a lot of the women walked. Not all but many. Maybe even most. Men could hardly help but watch the sway of their ass. When women walk like this, is this—in your opinion—just the way they happen to walk? Seems unlikely. How could they possibly know exactly what they look like from behind to have the maximum, calculated effect upon men? Do girls get together and practice their walks?

Nancy's response: They may not know exactly what they look like from behind, but they know men are watching and they certainly know that this is getting their attention. I don't think they'd practice it with others, since women are too competitive. They might when they're younger. When I did all the admin work for our European office, I shared an office with two Italian girls who not only had the walk that you're talking about, but if there were a pole in the room, they probably would have used that, too. They were always working it in a way that made me feel like they believed you had to do that to get what you want. It was interesting to watch.

Pound for pound, women's legs are just as strong as men's legs. There was a study done a long time ago: Researchers found that men who were attracted to breasts tended to be athletic, outgoing, gregarious, and social. Men attracted to the lower body, specifically the leg, were introverted, intellectual, passive, shy. Elmer Batters, who was a great leg photographer, thought that men got into legs because their mothers weren't loving enough. He thought that when a child cried, a loving mother would pick him up and cuddle him to her breast, so he would get into breasts. But the mother who didn't nurture would leave the child on the ground and all he had was the legs. It's an interesting theory. [Dian Hanson]

It's, finally, not all that complicated:
"Breast-men" had warm mothers.
"Ass-men" had cold mothers.

*

I interviewed three dozen "women who love men who kill," and when I went into it, I had no idea the answer. I think I have an answer. They have certain things in common. All of the women I interviewed had been abused in their childhood: by their fathers, their parents, some of them sexually, most of them physically, all of them psychologically. A lot of them had been victims of domestic violence from their first marriages. When they got into a relationship with a man in prison for life or on death row, he was (even though this may sound weird) a safe relationship, because he couldn't hurt them. Another thing all the women have in common is that they are Catholic.

What do you make of that? The first thing that jumps to my mind is that there's a belief in redemption, that people can be saved.

I don't think so. [Sheila Isenberg, Q&A with Barbara Herman]

After trauma, what people know most deeply is what they don't want to know. Knowledge crawls through the unprotected places. [Peter Straub]

Donatich's attraction to Lerner is the love a boy good at technical things finds in an almost insolvable puzzle, while her love for him is the love broken pieces of a vase feel for the glue. And what if her vase ever becomes whole again? Will it still need his glue? [D. T. Max]

No one is ever cured of anything; that much seems obvious.

Which brings me to you.

III
———

THIS IS THE PART

WHERE YOU'RE

SUPPOSED TO SAY

YOU LOVE ME

Love at first sight:

Only two possibilities—

There is something deep within me that wants to hurt something deep within you.

There is something deep within me that wants to be hurt by something deep within you.

—the brutal economy of romance, in which one person's doom becomes two people's destinations. [Harrison]

Hiking, I stumbled.

Falling, I reached out for your hand and you recoiled, saying (either literally saying or saying with your eyes, I now can't remember), *How dare you pull me down with you.*

*

The central conflict in American romantic comedies is always the same: love vs. work. When is Audrey Hepburn going to stop chasing money and fall in love with that blond writer guy? When is Nic Cage going to give up his job as an angel and love Meg Ryan the way she wants to be loved? Will the intrepid housing developer halt the wrecking ball simply because the woman whom he loves slings Americanos and biscotti in the doomed hometown café? Of course. Of course he will. True love always wins. That's where the American romantic comedy ends. French romantic comedies take that notion as a given. The question for Truffaut, Cocteau, Carné,

Rohmer, Godard is not, Why love? The question is, Why her? [Smith]

—one of those films, often considered a French specialty, that take sex so seriously as to make you wonder why anyone would bother with it. [Scott]

There has never been a great film about sexual obsession that is not, to some degree or another, a comedy. [Bruce Reid]
This is so obviously wrong I don't know what to say.
Nothing's more serious than sex.

*

We had just gotten engaged and this trip to Manzanillo was supposed to be a prenuptial honeymoon of sorts, so, for recreation you lay, like a virgin sacrifice, across the kitchen counter and confessed that the only fantasy you'd ever had was to open your legs as wide as you could and, under virtually gynecological scrutiny, be admired. Just that. So female. Be admired. You leaned back. Your bikini bottoms flapped about your ankles. I got into position.

When we were first married, being married struck me as equivalent to writing with my watch on (in a way that I loved); now I'm not sure what I'd compare it to exactly.

I've always preferred younger friends, idolizing girlfriends.
Why did I marry you?
I tell myself I thought you loved me, whereas I knew I'd wind up worshipping you.
(I wasn't in love with you when we got married, but I am now, whereas I suspect the opposite is true for you.)

In previous relationships, women would look to me to take care of them.

I was supposed to be the strong, silent, competent, sane one.

My reaction was always, pretty much, You're not serious.

Only you and I know the real story—which, of course, is never the same story.

My ego is so much more brittle than yours. Whenever we play Scrabble or Ping-Pong or pool or poker, I have to win. I need the nearly constant validation. You already know how great you are and dare me to tell you differently.

(You dare me to love you.)

*

I love how you say *Yum* with a nearly but not quite inaudible question mark at the end.

Love at 425 degrees. [Papa Murphy's Pizza]
Food, they say is, love.
So, they should say, is everything else.

In a very public display of presumed rivalry in 2008, singer and actress Jessica Simpson appeared with her then boy-friend, Dallas Cowboys quarterback Tony Romo, wearing a T-shirt that said REAL GIRLS EAT MEAT. Fans inter-preted it as a competitive dig at Romo's previous mate, Carrie Underwood, who is a vegetarian. [Cindy Meston]

I hate to say this, but I'd rather binge than make out. ["Heidi," Q&A with Mary Pipher]

When she and I walk into a restaurant, I watch grown men weep. [Donald Trump]

My mother said it was simple to keep a man: you must be a maid in the living room, a cook in the kitchen, and a whore in the bedroom. I said I'd hire the other two and take care of the bedroom bit. [Jerry Hall]

I had a rather delayed adolescence. One of the most embarrassing things I've ever done was, when the head cheerleader in seventh grade wanted to make out with me (I was incredibly cute as a kid), I declined because I was much more focused on demolishing an entire bag of lemon-crème cookies, about which no easy jokes or puns, please, Brenda.

And they will eat pizza and drink coffee, smoke cigarettes and be sweetly ignorant like two people who are about to fuck for the first time often are. [Joseph Salvatore]

You and I stage monthly dieting competitions, though neither of us is overweight.

Make breakfast wearing only an apron so I can get down on my hands and knees and eat you out from behind while you're cooking (the cook is mean—she whips the cream and beats the eggs).

*

In order to break through the numbness that they've learned, the only way they can feel is to hurt each other, at least initially. [Maggie Gyllenhaal]

You're nicer than I am.
Or: *I was just trying to be nice, but you don't like that—that doesn't work for you, that isn't what you like?*
Or: *I was just saying that to be mean.*

When Beecroft describes her life's dramatis personae, the word "mean" recurs as a leitmotif. She uses it of her mother, who raised her on a macrobiotic diet; of her angelic-looking half-sister; and of her "grave" and "soulful" young husband. He can sometimes be "as mean as possible, but I'm meaner to him. I tear men to pieces, so it's probably my fault." [Judith Thurman]

I seem too nice for mean girls to like me.
Mary Ann will always like me.
I will always be obsessed with Ginger.
Betty will always want to marry me.
I will always want to lick Veronica's boots.

*

I've worked in a ton of bookstores, including one in East Tennessee that sold romance novels—a whole wall of them—and they were extraordinarily graded and precise: the bodice-rippers ("historical romance") are long; the Silhouette romances, each one 120 pages long, offer specific imprints with specific degrees of carnality; the really dirty ones, or the dirtiest we had, were called *Velvet Glove*. [Jessica Burstein]

That the bookstores divide into romance and mystery suggests that the two most powerful fantasies are someone to love and someone to blame. [James Richardson]

—the continual game of Tag: You're It, also known as Tag: You Fucked Up.

No, really—what are your critiques of me? What are my supposed sins? Initiating sex without first negotiating about it ahead of time?

Why do you reflexively apply the diminutive "little" to everything you find endearing? Whence your need to infantilize me? Why do you take my emotional temperature only when you already know I'm in free-fall? Sometimes I wonder if you had all these skills before I entered your life, or have you had to acquire them as we went along?

That the man entertains even a single amorous inclination about this ball-breaker—much given to kittenish, come-hither comments along the lines of "Richard, I thought I asked you to tidy up" and "Why the hell can't you do something that needs doing?"—is testament to a libido of iron or to an erotic sensibility that leans toward the deeply masochistic. [Caitlin Flanagan]

Your brief description of this woman could be a pocket guide to abusive-relationship signs. [Hax]

I have scattered around my office so many photos of you.

Why don't you have a single photo of me anywhere in the house?

(You have photos of everyone else.)

I keep being on the verge of asking and then not asking.

(A gift requested is no longer a gift.)

She kept asking him over and over again, Did he like the present she had gotten him? Did he really, really like it? Would he use it? Did he want to try it out now? And he responded stiffly, irritably, with increasing distance. She behaved as if she wanted to win his love, but she was playing the loser so aggressively that it was almost impossible for him to respond with love or to respond at all. [Gaitskill]

Once, I asked Jack if he loved me.

"Of course I love you," he said.

"Then why don't you ever tell me?"

"It would be like having to tell you I'm breathing," he said. "It would be like if, in a movie, the hero turned to the woman just before they ran into a barrage of gunfire, took her hand, and said, 'Doris, I'm breathing.' I've always been breathing.

It would be like having her say, 'I know. I'm breathing, too.'"
[Linker]

The advice I'm dying to give to a girl walking down the street giving her boyfriend constant, reverential looks is, Don't—don't oversell the devotion.

*

Virginia Woolf wanted to know why women are so much more interesting to men than men are to women, but then that's Virginia Woolf.

I would say men and women don't desire each other equally, but then that's me.
Are you indifferent to me?
Repelled by me?
Repelled by your indifference?

In *Klute*, Jane Fonda says, looking at her watch, Fuck me. Ooh. Harder. Deeper.
That level of indifference.

*

Joke that my back doctor told me and that I then told you; you laughed, which was (continues to be?) evidence, to me, that our marriage wasn't (isn't?) over—
When the couple was first married, they were so lusty they had sex in every room in the house.
After several years, the passion died down a little, and they confined sex to the bedroom.
After many years, they passed each other in the hallway and said, Fuck you.

*

My stunning ex-student informs me that models are hired and fired strictly according to how many people buy the clothes they're wearing in the catalogue, compared to how many people buy the clothes when someone else is wearing the clothes in the catalogue.

I still want to read a serious book by someone who's extremely beautiful, about what it's like to go through life like that.

Is there such a book?

If so, I'm not aware of it.

I've suggested the idea over the years to a few male and female writers.

I try to say it in a substantial, un-awful way, but the pretty people still almost always look at me a little oddly.

Listening to two women behind me talk to each other about nothing in particular, I could immediately tell, to a virtual certainty, that the woman farthest away from me was beautiful and the woman closest to me was unattractive—based solely on the sound of their voices.

What would it be like to be that beautiful?

How does the world come to a person like that?

How does her beauty affect her perception of the world?

How does the world receive her?

The two people in a couple usually have approximately the same level of attractiveness, wouldn't you say?

—the sexiness, to me, of Marisa Acocella Marchetto's cartoon of two gorgeous women, one of whom is saying to the other, "Beauty is life's E-Z pass"; the sexiness lying in the punitive unfairness of it . . .

Four percent of women consider themselves beautiful.
[Jana Perez]

In all the years I've been a therapist, I've yet to meet one girl who likes her body. [Pipher]

The arrogance implied in believing that one's beauty can afford to be concealed is entrancing.

The same ex-student said to me, Some women truly like dick and some women don't—does your wife like dick?

*

What is the sexiest part of a man?
    His penis. No, right here [pointing to the spot between her hip and belly button]. What is this called?
    The Iliac crest.
    Oh my god. Will you make me sound smart and say the Iliac crest instead of the penis? I'll love you forever. [Kimberly Stewart, Q&A with David Keeps]

Your (ex-?)obsession with the patch of hair just above my belt.

Teeth—because blow jobs need to come with a gentle reminder of who's really in charge. [T-shirt worn by a déshabillé lady in Olympia]

Years into anyone's marriage, no one swallows cum—what does that tell us?

If I had a dick, you say, undoing my belt, *I'd make you suck it.*

*

I look to you for sympathy.
    You offer nonc.

Actually, not none.
Little.
A soupçon of fellow feeling.
Just enough to be the perfect amount?

If you make someone feel worthless often enough, he'll start to believe it.

Why am I the villain of every tale you tell?
Why do you think?
. . .
What was I going to ask you about?
Something to—
I forget.
. . .
You gotta stop it.
You gotta stop cloaking your manipulation in the rhetoric of concern.
Gaslight.

*

I'm confused by and addicted to your perpetual impulse to catastrophize, to disasterize.

Why do you always check to see how much I leave for a tip, study the passenger's side-view mirror the moment I turn on my right-side turn signal, always say I scared you when I come upon you unawares, feel compelled to comment upon how handsome you think Y is and how brilliant Z is, love to say (in response to my touch), *Down, boy,* never want to hold my hand in public, refuse to ever say *we*?
And yet—this is where it gets interesting—why do you always contrive to play the martyr?
So, too, of course, why do I allow you to maintain this stance?

You're quite self-centered and pretend not to be—which doesn't make you a hypocrite or a bad person.

It just makes you a person, full of the contradictions, internal dramas, and mysteries that everyone else has and that you have difficulty accepting about yourself.

You never, ever waver in your beliefs.

I don't get it.

I can't feel the humanness of you inside that certainty.

I can't not see certainty as anything other than the opposite of being alive.

(I suddenly get it: it's your mask.)

*

The sexiest things anyone does to anyone else are always selfish.

I mean, it's the selfishness itself that's sexy.

Women, asked to describe the best sexual experience of their lives, almost always mention an exceedingly brief thing they had decades ago with a near-convict.

Don't ask why.

(We all already know why.)

—your impossible-to-read tone, its irreducibly erotic faux-neutrality, its patient, slow valuelessness.

Sometimes I think you're perfectly awful, and sometimes I think you're expressing exquisite love by what you do for me—tightening the reins.

*

The advertisements, atop NYC cabs, for strip clubs frequently feature a highly exaggerated version of "bitch face."

Men are invited to either punish her for being a bitch or worship her for being a bitch.

The "bitch face" creates tension, which is relieved, briefly, by going to the strip club.

A smiling face would accomplish nothing.

When I say to you, *Tell me honestly,* you read in my eyes just how far you should go.

A black man is wearing a T-shirt that says DON'T BE A PUSSY. A white woman is wearing a T-shirt that says DON'T BE A DICK. I catch myself looking at this couple for longer than I should; they stare back daggers, and I can feel instantly the complications of such a relationship: how, even (especially) in virtue-signaling Seattle, it would be a very watchful relationship, very viewed in a way that would be erotic and exhibitionistic and exhausting.

You exhale and give me a nasty look.

The look is near-perfect.

It makes me both hostile and horny.

*

In my senior year of high school my best friend and I, who were both virgins, spent at least one night a week hanging around the San Francisco Airport. Why? The dirty magazines they let us flip through at the newsstand and the sexy "stewardesses" tugging their luggage like dogs on a leash, but more than that it was everybody marching with such military urgency to their destinations, as if everywhere—everywhere in the world: Winnipeg, Tunis, Cincinnati—were to be desired.

In an Amsterdam sex shop, I watched a videotape that consisted of nothing but a blonde woman repeatedly fondling and kissing and stroking and posting up and down on and generally worshipping an enormous, dark-colored dildo. One could feel, in the woman's impossibly adoring gaze, how precisely the tape had been niche-marketed for consumption by dark-colored men all over the planet (so, too, for white men fetishizing such dark-colored men).

She is straddling it, sucking on a string of pearls. [Carole Maso]

You saw an ad in *Harper's* for a vibrator; when the box arrived, I recognized the company's name and suggested that we use the vibrator together. You declined, saying it was only for you.

—Vanessa del Rio simultaneously sucking off six guys in a boxing gym's locker room; I watched this movie in a theater in the Combat Zone, before returning to the Boston suburb where I was staying at a very gynocentric "artists' colony" and where I met you.

In American vernacular, to say something "sucks" means servicing someone is no fun; getting serviced is the only fun; all that matters is who's doing whom; all that matters is who worships whom; all that matters is who's in control.

I've had this discussion with many men. Man to man: Is oral sex important to you?

No, it's not important to me. [Trump, Q&A with Howard Stern]

Mr. Weitz understands the nastiness that lurks within sweet, passive men; so does Mr. Braff. You get the feeling that this actor is ready to perform delicate surgery on some classically amiable character's heart of darkness. [Ben Brantley]

—a lovingly inscribed copy of *The Reluctant Submissive's Handbook* placed backward on the bookshelf. [Leanne Shapton]

She did not have the courage to stop doing what she wanted to do. She knew that it would not make her happy, because only the dreams of crazy people come true. [Jane Bowles]

The only thing that's sexy to me is what hurts.
I hate that.
I hate it.

Ballet adage: If it doesn't hurt, you're doing it wrong.
(I want it to hurt more.)

*

The conversation (ongoing, never ending) between my tongue and your pussy:

You must think that thing between your legs is lined with gold. [Robert Getchell]

Line of dialogue in Michaels's *Diaries*: "Lick the insides of my legs while I make this call."

One of the worst and, to me, most potent pop-song lines ever: the Eurythmics' "I want to dive into your ocean."

Life and relationship coach Shannon Ethridge encourages wives to keep their legs shaved and vaginas douched at all times. Just in case. [Dagmar Herzog]

I will do pretty much anything to view women perched on clear, plastic high heels, pussy-shaped pedestals on which they 1) struggle to stand and 2) are worshipped.

In Mary Karr's formulation, an elongated foot and leg announce that "there's pussy at the other end of this" and "I'm a woman who can not only take an ass-whipping; to draw your gaze, I'll inflict one on myself."

The only thing I've ever liked about Bill Clinton is that Gennifer Flowers said he eats pussy like a "champ"—such a fantastic word, in context.

The only thing I've ever found noteworthy about Marv Albert was his attempt to come up to a colleague in a hotel room and fall to his knees in front of her. She filed charges, as well she should have, but he was there to express his worship of the human body—which, as a pseudo-caustic sportscaster, he's spent his entire adult life ridiculing.

Postcard left in my university mailbox the month my book *Black Planet: Facing Race during an NBA Season* was published:

Mitty miscreant, Bravo! You've completed the weak circle left arcing at the lame end of Jump Shot. The one thing your book doesn't do is contain vitality, uninhibited sensuousness, the kind that Gary Payton might exhibit when licking pussy. Even if you could hit a jump shot, you could never lick anything without your drab self-consciousness wandering around bedside, turning everything into a limp masturbation party. You'll never lick my pussy, even though I know you'd like to. You didn't pass the audition.

Women are not pure, and they know it is why the middle smells so good. [Carson]

It ain't gonna lick itself.

Line of dialogue in *Wedlocked*: "Keep your hand poised at the center of desire that lies just outside my pussy."

This is what you taste like.
Sweetheart—like no one has ever said that before.

*

The disappearing hair of women: First it was neatened up. Then it became a kind of thick landing strip. Then a less thick strip. Then a little mouse toupee. Then an eyelash. Then . . . nothing.

Victoria's Secret's (the location of Victoria's secret is indicated by the first letter of her name) seemingly never-ending PINK RULES campaign: nine-year-old girls walking around saying, more or less, PUSSY RULES.

Pink is associated with girls because it's the color of their pussies; blue is associated with boys because it's the color of the veins in their cocks.

Women today shave many parts of their body for some obvious reasons. If you plan on wearing shorts or a skirt, of course you're going to shave your legs. If you have dark arm hair, you may shave that hair. Some women even shave their upper lip (which isn't a good idea; you should always go with waxing when it comes to that area). And of course we shave our bikini lines when we go to the beach. But there wasn't always such a need for shaving anywhere near our pubic area. [Carol Lwali]

—at a strip club in Portland, a woman wearing a T-shirt that says I HAVE THE PUSSY, SO I MAKE THE RULES.

Before the 1980s, women didn't really shave around their vaginal area at all. That era's swimsuits covered the bikini line area pretty well (they were a little like the boy-shorts women wear today), so there wasn't a need for it. But when the '80s-style bikinis, with a thinner strip of material between the legs, became popular, women started to worry about their pubic hair poking out of the sides of these skimpier suits, so they started to shave their "bikini lines," as we call that area today. [Lwali]

Juicy Couture. [Authentic Brands Group]

This is still a long way from what women do now, however. Girls today act as if not shaving their pubic hair is a sin. To have hair down there is viewed as dirty and vulgar, and letting it grow out is just letting yourself go and showing that you don't care how you look. However, these girls would be very surprised if they knew exactly what started the whole craze of shaving pubic hair. [Lwali]

Mickey Rooney on Ava Gardner: She had this little extra—it was like a little warm mouth—that would reach up and grab me and take me in and make my, uh, my heart swell.

Long ago, prostitutes shaved their pubic hair, possibly as a way to avoid getting crabs, so other women would never even consider doing such a thing, but the invention of the VHS is what ultimately would start the trend as it exists today. [Lwali]

Thank you.
For what?
Did you shave your pussy for me?
Uh uh—I'm going swimming.

In the '80s, sadomasochism, or S&M, or SM, became very popular. SM porno VHS tapes were readily available, and since men could watch them in the comfort of their own homes, sales took off. In these videos, women were often portrayed as being very weak. One of the ways they tried to make themselves look weaker was by shaving their pubic hair. This made them appear completely naked, child-like, and extremely vulnerable. The look became popular with fans of the tapes, and men probably started convincing their girlfriends to imitate the look. Girls who were fans of the videos also followed suit. This was not as widespread a phenomenon as it is today, though. It was more of a cult movement. That is, until *Playboy* decided to imitate the look. [Lwali]

—lip gloss to make men think about vaginas. [Gold]

Thirty seconds to three minutes before a woman has an orgasm, her labia redden.

John McCain to Cindy McCain, after she mocked his thinning hair: At least I don't plaster on the makeup like a trollop, you fucking cunt.

"Cunt," as used in Britain, is a far harsher word than "pussy." It signifies intransigence, malignity, and all-out shittiness. [Jonathan Raban]

While women today think the '90s was when the look became popular, the first *Playboy* centerfold featuring a shaved vagina didn't take place until about 2002. Eventually, *Playboy* started using the look in all of its photo shoots. This is when the fad really took off. Strippers and women in the adult entertainment industry probably were some of the first to follow the trend, since they needed to be aware of what men were into sexually, and it just continued to expand until it became the norm with women in the US. [Lwali]

You're closed so tight—do you ever loosen up? [Steven Shainberg]

But the idea that anyone should do these exercises because her pussy isn't tight enough is crazy. It's a very effective way to ruin her sex life. And it's the same thing if a woman tells a man, You can't satisfy me because your penis is too small.

That's like saying, You can't satisfy me because you have red hair or because you're only five foot five. If the "reason" has something to do with your body, there's not a whole lot you can do about it. [Bright]

Bernie Madoff's mistress has a new book out detailing her affair with everyone's most hated financial advisor. She notes that he has a small penis, and while that didn't seem to inhibit their sexual pleasure, she mentions it partially, I assume, in revenge for his treatment (emotional and financial) of her, and partly because she thinks it may somewhat explain his personality. Did Madoff's grandiosity emanate at all as compensation for his small penis? Did he know that his wealth would help women overlook the fact that he was underendowed? She seems to think so. Or was he naturally arrogant, insidious, and pathologically unconcerned with the welfare of others? Would he have behaved exactly as he did if he had a very large penis? [Pepper Schwartz]

Once the penis enters the vagina, the woman becomes emotional, which is obviously such a cliché but probably true enough. [Phillips]

Romantic love is associated with elevated activity of the neurotransmitters dopamine and norepinephrine. Attachment is associated with the hormones oxytocin and vasopressin. [Lori Gottlieb]
Seminal fluid has all of these chemicals in it. If you don't want to fall in love, don't have sex. [Helen Fisher]

Women today shave because they think it's sexy and it's the look that's "in" right now. Little do they realize that they're imitating a look that became popular because it made women look weak and submissive. [Lwali]

Smoke a cigarette (your former vice) while I lick your shaved pussy; put your hand on the back of my head, talk to me, guide me, praise me.

*

In the *Bhagavad Gīta,* the human body is defined as a wound with nine openings.

I'm forced to concede that I adore wounds. [Hervé Guibert]

Most married adults—male and female—know something about the business of trading intensity for security and passion for comfort. But as wistful as they may sometimes grow for the excitements of yesteryear, very few of them have the mettle to live out Bentley's austere choice [foregoing romantic relationships in favor of anal-sex assignations]. Her desire and ability to do so may, she acknowledges, be evidence of deep psychic wounds. If so, she is happy to be wounded. [Zoë Heller]

Fifty Shades of Grey—male dominance, female submission—is (was) culturally acceptable, but male powerlessness is (still?) offensive.

Vonnegut, pretending not to know the answer, asks, Why are American men obsessed with golf and blow jobs?

You're replacing the bathroom sink. You're trying to pry the old one loose. I lift the old one off, which you couldn't quite do. I've always liked Rocky Balboa's line about Adrian: "She fills gaps." There are distressingly few gaps I fill for you, since you're so handy, so seemingly self-sufficient. For once I feel, acutely, the pleasure of doing something physically that you can't do yourself.

(This passage now feels dated, alluding as it does to my supposedly superior strength, which no longer exists.)

More than 50 percent of respondents report having fantasies in which an authoritative woman, often a nurse or a teacher, behaves in a sexually aggressive fashion. Straight men interested in erotic submission far exceed the number of women willing to dominate them. Men's interest in taking a passive, submissive, or masochistic sexual role remains one of the most taboo subjects in our culture. [Lauren M. E. Goodlad (!?)]

Rather like stuttering or homosexuality, masochism doesn't fit easily into the overall upward swing of human progress. Is it only rationalization on my part to view masochism as a commendable stymying of the survival-of-the-fittest narrative?

And yet I can't read the *Stranger* or listen to sports radio talk show host Mitch Levy, because in each case it's too transparently obvious what the newspaper's and show's MO is: to make the audience cringe/cower/squirm. Levy (recently arrested and fired for solicitation) is overtly sadistic, saying, "Can you imagine a worse loss than the Seahawks' loss to the Patriots? How much does it hurt?" I adore his colleague Dave Mahler, who leans into the pain, loves it, lives for it ("I don't get over anything, ever").

Because:

The only music I've ever really loved is lamentation. What else is there to say about anything?

*

Halfway through my appearance, I had Colbert on the defensive and the audience on my side "against" him, but lacking the killer instinct, I pulled back; he pounced, mercilessly.

The con man does give you something. It is a sense of your own worthlessness. [George W. S. Trow]

Some people will do anything to get away from a camera—just look at you; some people will do anything to get in front of a camera—just look at me. (Joke my mom liked to tell: "Anti-Semitism has held me back in my field." "What field?" "R-R-Radio.")

In the end, however, it is often the case that others use us only as we have invited them to. [Hax]

In a meeting with me and my editor and the publicity department, my then agent, as a way to inveigle himself with the publisher, repeatedly if subtly belittled me and my work.

Even though I begged you not to tell your parents that I lost one hundred dollars on back-to-back bets in a game of three-card monte on 42nd Street, you gleefully told them the moment we got back to their hotel on Central Park South, and then they, of course, told all their friends, one of whose children used the story as an irrelevant flashback in a horrendously bad screenplay he wrote.

*

You love action males and their mastery of complex, explosive machinery, even as they pose a threat to you. Your family hides behind these men; these men hide behind their secrecy.

The subtitle of Ross McElwee's documentary *Sherman's March* is "A Meditation on the Possibility of Romantic Love in the South During an Era of Nuclear Weapons Proliferation," which sounds like a joke, only it's not. The camera becomes a heat-seeking missile that destroys whatever it touches.

I've never liked guns or weapons of any kind. I'm not looking here for praise or credit. I'm wondering what my masculinity consists of, exactly, absent worship of equipment.

Unless I make a conscious attempt to deepen my voice, when I call down to the front desk to ask for, say, a foam pillow, the hotel operator is as likely as not to address me as "Ma'am."

*

When people see a strong horse and a weak horse, by nature they will like the strong horse. [Osama bin Laden]

Will is what counts between animals, as between most humans. [Gray]

Nothing is more off-putting to me (and sexier) than your will to power.

—how surprised and embarrassed I felt when you said, *Five years in, I realized you wanted to be pushed around.*

I didn't know how to respond.

I still don't.

I don't want you to know that about me, which may mean I don't actually want to do as much as I pretend I want to do about any of this.

How did I get designated to "work hard" in sex while you do nothing?

Why do you keep asking me to dress up in your clothes? (You ask again, keep asking; you say, quasi-jokingly, *I may need to punish you further.*)

Why did you ask me to clean up my piss on the bathroom floor while you were still sitting on the toilet?

Why am I getting hard writing all this down right now?

You like being in charge; I like being your handmaiden.

Sorry I'm not doing anything.

It's okay. The only thing you have to do to be good in bed is show up.

After we weary of my paying homage to one part of your body (e.g., your eyebrows—sometimes for months at a time), we move onto another body part (e.g., your shoulders).

You're ignoring my feet.

Tarantino and pretty feet: [Dargis]
a high arch, a wide instep, and a staircase-like progression of toes. [Gottlieb]
—the red vinyl chair across from the toilet on which he sits her down and kneels before her pussy like a supplicant, like Mary Magdalene kneeling before Jesus to bathe his dirty feet. [Ponteri]

The world is full of guys who are lost and scared. One of my favorite correspondents—I have a lot of letters from him—offered his skin to me so I could have it made into shoes. He wrote me, "I am an ordinary man. Ordinary height. Ordinary looks. Women never look at me. I'm invisible. But women love shoes. If I were a pair of shoes, women would want me. I fantasize about being a pair of shoes." [Hanson]

I need to believe you hate me and go to bed with me only because you have to.

She loved Johnson, but his neediness must have been claustrophobia-inducing. [Gopnik]

Does my passivity secrete your hostility/aggression?
Of course it does, but to what extent and which generated which?
Did I instinctively know you would turn out to be my unraveling, and protest though I might, do I not crave this disintegration?

Can we talk now?
What's the matter, sweetie? You have that look on your face.

92

Let's face it.
Face what?

Did I seek you—a woman of your icy temperament—by accident?

On purpose?

Did I instinctively know you were this way, would become this way?

You became this way on purpose, because you knew this is what I wanted?

Do I love you despite or because of your nastiness toward me?

(Not even a question.)

*

When *Vogue* asked me to write about a fetish, I wanted to come up with something more interesting/surprising than fishnet stockings or French braids.

Having said so, I became so: I'm now obsessed with severely pretty women (e.g., you) wearing glasses.

In glasses, you look perfect.

Desire is indistinguishable for me from distance.

When I said, over and over again, *Look back at me in the mirror,* you said, each time, *Pardon me?*

—the (pseudo-documentary) depilatory scene in *The 40-Year-Old Virgin*; the (oblique but legible) joke in *Bridesmaids* about men and the inevitable discovery of their paraphilias.

In effect, I'm married to Margaret Dumont (you don't get my jokes); the awful comedy of this.

*

I love you.
    Silence.
    Do you want to know if I love you?

    Or:
    I'm not sure I'm in love with you anymore—do you think I am?

    Or:
    I love you. . . . This is the part where you're supposed to say you love me.
    I know.
    Do you pity-love me?

    Or:
    I want more life.
    I don't.
    Are we too different?
    I don't think so—I don't know.
    I love the world more than you do.
    I don't love the world at all.
    Do you ever feel safe outside?
    I don't know—do you ever feel safe inside?

*

Whom have you had crushes on?
    David Strathairn. Hugh Grant. David Foster Wallace. David Gates. Dave Eggers.
    WASPy rascals, most of whom are named David or Dave.
    Taylor Kitsch. Robert Taylor. Todd Rundgren. James Taylor. Paul Rudd.
    Long-haired layabouts, most of whom are named Taylor. . . . When I mentioned gay men's obsession with the clean-cut, straight-edge look, for some reason you felt compelled to say—
    I remember what I said.

Tell me what you like.
Or: Tell me what your previous lovers were like.
Or: I can always tell when you're fantasizing about someone else.

—the fantasy that I pay you for sex.

Shrink: Tell me your sex fantasies and I'll tell you who you are.

I'll tell you who I was thinking of if you'll tell me who you were thinking of.
You don't want to know.

When I waxed rhapsodic once over a snaky-haired masseuse, you countered with a memory of a guy with an astonishingly thick dick.

*

I'm reading Pete Townshend's autobiography right now. I used to like his music, and I've always identified with him. I far prefer his workaholic self-loathing to Keith Richards's knife-wielding self-love, which simply doesn't register for me.

Is self-loathing a requirement for writers? Thomas Mallon and Anna Holmes discuss the role of self-hatred in creativity. [*The New York Times Book Review*]

Human nature is so constructed that it gives affection most readily to those who seem least to demand it.
In love, there is always one who kisses and one who offers the cheek.
Love is a spaniel that prefers even punishment from one hand to caresses from another.

She who would long retain her power must use her lover ill.

To abuse a man is a lover-like thing and gives him rights.

There is one woman whom fate has destined for each of us; if we miss her, we are saved.

The love that lasts the longest is the love that is never returned.

The Lovers Quotation Book is a Rorschach test.

Every statement that makes my heart fall is an inkblot of agony/anger.

IV

PORN

AN INTERLUDE

In American movies, in contests between thoughtful analysis and inchoate feeling, inchoate feeling always wins out.

Sentimentality always pimps for hostility; morality always screens voyeurism.

The camera is always doing to the damsel-in-distress's ass what the bad-guys-in-the-plot are judged in the harshest possible terms for trying to do.

In *Deep Throat,* Linda Lovelace's friend (a Rita Moreno look-alike) lifts up a guy's chin while he's eating her out and asks, "Mind if I smoke while you're eating?"

Patsy Carroll, a school friend of Linda's, saw the film, went home, and wept. She says, "I just felt like someone I loved had died." [Anthony Lane]

Although Bob was an FBI agent, he looked up to Jack, whom he viewed as a real man because he had served in Vietnam and had far greater sexual experience. Bob fantasized about what it would be like for Jack to have sex with Bonnie. These were fantasies, since both men knew that Bonnie didn't feel comfortable around Jack, didn't like his extended visits to their home, and would never entertain the possibility of such ideas in the first place. They remained, instead, part of the ongoing exchange of pornography across the Atlantic between two old high school friends who never really left the adolescent phase of their infatuation with sex. Since Bonnie would not have allowed herself to be swapped between friends, Bob invited Jack on numerous occasions to do the next best thing: secretly watch husband and wife make love. Without Bonnie's knowledge, Bob asked Jack to watch them from a deck outside their bedroom. Later, Bob installed a secret video camera in the bedroom of their northern Virginia home so Jack could watch them on a monitor in another part of the house via closed-circuit video. Jack hadn't asked to watch Bob and Bonnie in bed; it was always at Bob's invitation. Bob wanted to show Jack what a fantastic lover he was and what an incredible woman Bonnie became between the sheets. [David Vise]

For the vast majority of the male viewing audience, porn "fails" without at least the pantomime of female sexual pleasure. Without it, no scopophilia. If porn is to be believed, most men are as preoccupied with female desire as we are unaware of what it is we really want. [Alain Robbe-Grillet]

Even when a window looks out onto water, I usually pull the shade.

I've never been a big fan of a view.

*

Men don't speak up and demand what they want. They accept this Faustian bargain: they can have all the sexual entertainment they want, but only if they agree to keep their mouth shut and accept guilt and shame. They think, If I were a better person, I wouldn't need this; I must be awfully lonely; I must be awfully ugly; I must be awfully insecure to have to resort to this terrible vice. [Bright]

In Kafka's story "First Sorrow," the trapeze artist wants to live up on the trapeze his entire life.

Then he has his first sorrow.

His first sorrow is that he wants to add a second trapeze bar.

He's getting awfully lonely up there all by himself.

*

Falling in love—that phenomenon of emotional life described with clinical chill by Freud as "sexual overestimation" . . . . [Joyce Carol Oates]

Why do people flip each other off?

Why do they say, "Fuck you"?

It is very difficult to say that there is a major distinction in the level of sex involved between being assaulted by a penis and being assaulted by a fist, especially when the perpetrator is a man. [MacKinnon]

Is sex really that awful?

Is the dick that abhorrent? ("Does your wife like dick?")

Human beings are not a very loving species, especially when they make love. [Stoller]

In *Toward the End of Time*, the impotent Ben Turnbull recalls when he could still "shoot semen into a woman's wincing face like bullets of milk." [John Updike]

Everyone is either a victim of a sexual crime or the perpetrator of a sexual crime or a therapist treating sexual crimes. . . . She tells me how she became a therapist. She went to visit her own therapist once, he questioned her openness, and she wound up doing golden showers in his office. . . . That, she tells me, is why men like fat women. They will do anything. Name your fantasy. Try out your imagined humiliation. [Charles Bowden]

When waitresses who are "nice" suddenly start acting "mean," their tips almost always increase dramatically.

No one will ever love you passionately for being nice.
[Charles Baxter]

Porn actress Kendra Lust, qua high school biology teacher,
tells a father—who complains that his son is being bullied—
that the kid is just a pussy. Then when the father is down on
all fours, licking her pussy, she says, "You can't get enough of
it, can you? Aaaawww." It's the way she stretches out the last
word that makes my body go cold.

*

According to you, many women masturbate to the rape scene
in *The Accused*.

Women's desire is not relational but narcissistic. It's dominated by yearning for self-love, by the wish to be the object of
erotic admiration and sexual need. [Marta Meana]
What women want is a real dilemma: they want to be
cared for; they want to be overpowered. [Daniel Bergner]
At least 1 in 10 women fantasize about sexual assault at
least once per month in a pleasurable way. [Meana]

How do I parse that and still want love—the body's ceaseless yearning?
I'm serious:
How could anything ever possibly work between men and
women?

*

He takes the subway to a banged-up-looking block, maybe in
Hell's Kitchen, climbs up to his tiny, soiled apartment, nothing on the walls but a few pinups, women torn from magazines. [Mark Doty]

In my local convenience store, cigarette ads with open-mouthed women are hung just inside the door at, I never fail to notice, crotch level.

You're pretty.
Thanks.
Beautiful, even.
You should see me with your dick in my mouth.

But there was something a bit cruel in the mouth, and the eyes were cold. [Ian Fleming's description of James Bond]

I went through a Seka phrase—did any straight American man not, in the early eighties, go through a Seka phase?—until I noticed that, in group shots with other women, Seka was granted the rare privilege of not having to make eye contact with the viewer; even for me, this seemed too remote a spot from which to worship the goddess. The fantasy was that she disdained me until I fucked her into admiring me.

*

Then the boy replays a porno film, paid for / a quarter at a time, bad milk spilled in a booth. [Roger Fanning]

They have lots of janitors with mops who are constantly running in and cleaning up. Some guys clean up after themselves and some don't, but these mop-up crews keep pretty busy; at least in the better places they do. When I first started going to adult theaters I had this fear of fluids, but it wasn't as bad as I thought. Some places have this unaccountable odor. I don't know what causes it. [Bright]

In the 1990s, when the man behind the counter at the "adult" movie store asked if he could help me find something, I said, "Just browsing."

He replied, "That's what I said four years ago, and look at me now."

*

At Green Lake Park I stand behind a bush to pee for a long time. A woman, walking by with her boyfriend, thinks I'm masturbating with her in mind. When they drive away, she yells at me, "I hope it was worth it!"

I'd just masturbated before making love with you the time you got pregnant; I worried a little what effect (if any) that might have on our child-to-be's DNA. I even went so far as to ask a pregnancy-and-childbirth book author, who reassured me that if anything this would improve the motility of the sperm—which, of course, provided little surcease for my worrying mind.

How can I look at this picture and masturbate? For all I know, this woman might be a racist. She might be a child-beater. She might be a meat-eater. She might be mean to her cats. How do we know what she's really like? One could have these fantasies and perhaps feel insecure about them: Am I a cruel person? Do I believe in these stereotypes and prejudices? One may get to a point where one feels quite confident and says, "Well, as a matter of fact, I don't." [Bright]

It's one definition of pornography: whatever we will not talk about. [Tisdale]

—porn: the world's one true religion.

—Molly Parker looking at herself in the mirror and saying, "I have the hottest, wettest, tightest pussy." It's a quote from some book about stripping that girls use to pump themselves up. [Wayne Wang]

The drama of a woman's pleasure is written not on her genitals but her face. [Lisa Katzman]

—money shot: a woman winking at the camera while she's swallowing.

What, to me, is so sexy about it?

The detachment.

Two porn conventions I don't get: the woman slapping her own clit to get things going and her spitting on the head of his cock.

It's no good without Mister Monster. You must have Mister Monster. [Amis]

In porn, why does the man always come on the outside? What's the point? I believe he came. [Bright]

I like to be peed on. I like being spat on. It feels like cum on your chest. I like to be choked. I like to be fisted. A girl can have sixteen fingers up her, but no thumbs. For vaginal I prefer a girthy kind of dick. For anal I prefer a longer, thinner kind of dick.

So when you do DP, you get one thick one and one thin one?

Right. No. Come to think of it, I get two thick ones. I like to feel crammed. ["Chloe," Q&A with Amis]

In *The Kids Are All Right,* Annette Bening and Julianne Moore watch gay male porn together, and when their son catches them, they explain that women's sexual organs are internal, so they sometimes need to watch gay male porn to get themselves aroused, because it's erotic to see sexual organs manifest.

Porn shows everything without comment. Here it is: Here's a cock and a pussy jumping up and down on each

other. Here's what sucking looks like. And here's what somebody's big fat butt looks like. It's all right there. It doesn't try
to make anything other than what it is. It's a language everyone knows but no one wants to acknowledge. It's like yelling,
"Fuck," in a crowded movie theater. [Bright]

When Brenda's computer crashed, she received a CD of
every image she'd ever looked at on the computer, including
every porn image.

She asked me what I thought she should do with the
images.

I knew but couldn't bring myself to say.

My computer kept freezing, my computer consultant kept
coming over to fix it, and I think both you and I knew/sus-
pected what the underlying cause was.

What's the matter with you? you asked me when I wanted
to make out at midnight in the village square of your New
England hometown. *Are you looking at porn on the internet all
the time?*

You can't know (or maybe you do) how incredibly erotic
the photos of just your mouth are. What is it about not seeing
your eyes that makes those pictures so sexy?

The lure of glory-hole anonymity.

In Amsterdam sex shops, I was struck mainly by the
arrangement of movies and magazines into exceedingly min-
ute subdivisions of pleasure and pain.

Let's say that all instances of using gendered language per-
petuate sexism not only within the political realm but within
the personal realm as well. For instance, when I tell a group
of peers, "I wish she would just quit being a bitch," what I'm
really doing is punishing a woman for being assertive and
thus reinforcing the sexist norm established by a patriarchal

system. And even when I just wish someone would quit being such a bitch, I'm perpetuating the idea in my own brain that a woman shouldn't be assertive, thus reinforcing my own patriarchal impulses. Let's also say that many of the women with whom I have sex define themselves as staunch feminists who demand that the public not use gendered language and who struggle for equality in social and domestic arenas—all while suffering from a range of sexual discrimination and violence. And let's say as well that I, too, am a staunch feminist who buys the argument that perpetuating sexism in any way is an all-around bad idea. And so then why would you say—in the most intimate setting imaginable, when we are at our most Pavlovian—that you want me to come on your face and chest as if you were a towel? Why would you say, "I like to be on top when I'm with other men, but I'd like you on top of me"? Or "I want to be dominated"? Or "Do you think it's sexy when I tear up? Say you think it's sexy when I tear up." "It might be hot if you say, 'That's a good girl,' and stuff like that. Tell me you want me to suck your dick. Tell me you want to gag me. Why are men so quiet when they're fucking? Wrap your hands around my neck and fuck me, you idiot." [Smith]

In the *Tattoo* magazine supplement to the New Orleans tattoo convention, an inordinately buxom but somehow slightly demure-looking blonde babe is on the cover, wearing a sailor hat, fishnet stockings, a short red skirt, white gloves, a bra top, and a couple of tattoos. Behind her in black shadow is a dark-haired woman dressed in a leopard costume. The function of the blonde babe's tattoo is to portray her in the process of being transfigured from sailor-girl to jungle-cat and back again (and to portray as well the eros of this tension between civilization and savagery).

You usually lighten your hair, but one time the hairdresser darkened it a little and it looked great; you asked me how I liked it. I was thinking, Make it even blacker—make it jet-black.

*

I would call the LA-look designer plastic or name-brand trash. Those girls pay good money to look cheap. The last time I was down there, I bought a T-shirt that said THEY'RE REAL; I felt like I was the only one in town who didn't have enhancement surgery. . . . Women in LA definitely have their own way of dressing—one step above hooker. They really accentuate their asses. [Nancy Williams]

One year in LA, in my late twenties, immediately after the breakup of a relationship, I became a huge fan of a massage parlor out in the Valley called Misfits. I never went there, but I loved looking at their ad in the phone book, loved thinking about the perfect pun of their name: Miss/Fits (a little relief in a tight spot for the alienated man).

I love women, but a part of me was hurt by my mother and I wonder if her unavailability is the reason I enjoy seeing women in compromising situations on film and if anger and fantasies are sometimes synonymous. I am relieved by your non-hysterical attitude toward sex and would appreciate any suggestions from you. [letter from "Mark" to advice columnist Jennifer James]

I was supposed to give a little ticket that I held in my hand to the woman of my dreams, but instead I got up and gave the ticket to the only masseuse who was not in any way appealing or exciting or terrifying.

Leaving the massage parlor, I felt the same way I'd felt upon leaving the theater after seeing a pornographic movie for the first time: sentimental, thrilled by the mundanity of cracks in the sidewalk and flowers, and repelled by the prospect of physical love.

I kept asking the woman in the peep show to do this, mouth that, look a certain way, until she finally said, "What do you want, a girlfriend or a show?"

The highlight of the show, for me, was her rubbing her middle finger over the money slot as if it were her clit, then pressing her ass up against the plexiglass in front of my face while waving my five-dollar tip at the next guy on her rounds.

*

Your eyes are always slammed shut in sex.

When asked what they visualize when they climax, few men say it's the partner they're with. [Peter Kramer]

Married men masturbate more than single men.

You look good in sunglasses.
Thanks.
Because they hide your eyes.
Got it.
I can't think of anyone else who has such sad eyes.

*

David Milch, TV producer/notorious sadist (abused, of course, when he was a kid)/quondam creative writing teacher—after reading a story I wrote in which the protagonist 1) is teased by his friends and ministered to by his parents and 2) makes love with his girlfriend and watches porn—asked me to identify in each set the one that demonstrated genuine love, and I answered both times, in his view, incorrectly.

The room is fluorescent purple Plexiglas. Black light dominates. A woman—wearing a bathing suit composed of neongreen straps—dances around a pole. Her hair is bleached blond, flat-ironed. We gather around the circular stage and order Dr. Peppers. She lures me onto the stage by curling her finger. I practically float up to her. She slides her hands across my shoulders and begins to dance around me as if I were the pole. My friends shout and throw dollars all over the place. She reaches around my hips and unbuckles my pants, pulling them down and revealing to the crowd that I'm wearing oversized, neon-yellow boxers that feature penguins wearing Santa hats. At the sight of my boxers, my friends shout and flash more money. The black light makes their teeth glow bright white with purple edges. I think this woman wants me to have sex with her in front of everyone. Performance anxiety sets in. She pushes on my back with one hand, which I take as an instruction to get down on all fours. She straddles me and sits on my back. Then she folds my belt over and whips the hell out of me, growling, "Tell me you like it." She whips me some more. "Tell me you like it," she insists. She's talking directly to me, in a low tone. No one else can hear. This isn't part of the show. [Smith]

Forty years ago—my freshman year of college—I put a quarter in a booth in a Times Square porn palace, and the curtain came up on a man and woman fucking. I thought the glass window was up but just unusually transparent; in fact, it wasn't up. During a break in the action, the woman reached over the four-foot partition and tried to swat me.

*

Slim flees the house and eventually assumes another identity, moving first to Seattle, where she stays with Joe (Dan Futterman), a gentle ex-boyfriend, and then to Michigan. As she makes her way around the country, the movie purports to offer advice to battered wives. Most of it is very grim, and I wouldn't trust it for a second. The movie also offers an explanation for Slim's choice of a husband. An adopted child, she tracks down her biological father in Seattle to ask him for financial help. He turns out to be just like her ex-husband, Mitch, only 25 years older. As for Joe, who might have emerged as a hero in another version of the story, the movie baldly states that the gentle, handsome, nurturing friend wasn't enough of a man in bed to make Slim happy. Even Joe cheerfully admits it. [Stephen Holden]

Being with Paolo leads her to conclude that there is a relationship between the size of her lover's penis and her state of mind. A male director would take a barrage of flak for coming to comparable conclusions. [Maslin]

If you don't have anyone, the sexy, young television actress told the *SNL* audience, I'll be your valentine.

Sad to say, her condescension—her narcissism—got me hard.

(I didn't hate her because she was beautiful; I hated myself because I wasn't.)

Just as we size them up, they size us up, and they are actually quite good at distinguishing whether a woman is self-assured (or arrogant), sweet (or saccharine), and sharp-witted or (sharp-tongued). They may not use the same words, but they ferret out quickly if a woman is desperate, bitter, or incredibly hard to please. [sex advice column]

An indifferent woman wearing a lot of eye shadow sits in a glass booth.

Although the agreed-upon fiction is that she can't see my eyes in the black light, she faces me directly and asks, That's all you got?

(You gotta do something, I think; I'm a grow-er, not a show-er!)

*

As Peter Mountford, your fellow Scot, explained to me, "The origin of Scottish dourness is the weather and, even more so, the brutal history of subjugation and invasion. Also, Scots are notoriously frugal, probably because they had to live lean for so many centuries, under the boot of the English. To this day, after the stroke of midnight on New Year's Eve/Day, the first person allowed into your house, carrying a piece of coal and a bottle of whiskey, should be dark-haired (i.e., not a Viking). This tradition, known as 'first footing,' is done in most houses.

"The Scottish people are very rational and deliberate. They're unsentimental. They get weepy after they've had whiskey, but generally they dodge vivid emotion. Concerted thinking is weirdly commonplace in Scotland, and (very polite) arguments are everywhere, always heavy on reason and light on passion. Fundamentalism—political, religious—is rare. Maybe they got it out of their system with John Knox. In any case, there's a tendency not so much toward the center of issues as circumspection about anyone's firm position.

"A fundamental principle of economics is that we all want to maximize our utility. People always want more. No one wants less. To economists, daily life is about extending one's utility—one's take-away value in a given interaction. They have faith in reason. Life, though, doesn't conform to logic. At some point, despite our best efforts, we're all flying blind. Good economists know and accept this."

It is, to me, at times, as if you're a Dickens character named Mrs. Common-Sense.

Miserliness is, after all, one of the most reliable signs of profound unhappiness. . . . Nothing alive can be calculated. [Kafka]

Whenever I reread the précis for a poli-sci paper you wrote eons ago, I never fail to be moved by your belief/hope that the actions human beings take might be based to any degree whatsoever on rational thought.

—and yet your nearly invariable tendency to exaggerate dramatically whenever you're attempting to marshal an argument.

—the utterly dialectical nature of your intelligence, whereby you are incapable of hearing anything I say without needing to respond immediately with the antithesis.

Joke, courtesy of your cousin: Did you hear about the Scottish woman who loved her husband so much she nearly told him?

I lived for years in Ireland. The majority of intelligent Irishmen dislike Irishmen, and they're right. Every Irishman will tell you that. Seven hundred years of bitter oppression changed their character, gave them that passive meanness and cunning. When we were making *Othello,* I asked Micheál MacLiammóir to describe the Irish in one word. He said, "Malice." [Orson Welles]

A calm and collected soul, unruffled and kindly in manner, he was always impeccably dressed for his business engagements. One morning he turned up for his first meeting looking slightly disheveled, no tie, his collar undone, not serious lapses, but noticeable because uncharacteristic. Nevertheless, he went about the day's business in his usual mode, nothing else awry that subsequently anyone remembered, and when he'd worked through all his day's appointments, he went to the local police station and told the officer on duty that last night he'd murdered his wife when she was in bed. She'd told him he was mean, and by way of a response he'd suffocated her with a pillow. "Mean." It was the way she said it, I suppose. [Gray]

Does your personality consist of not brandishing a personality, of not possessing peculiarity?

I admire and pity your self-erasure.

(I love you when you babble to yourself in your sleep; I can feel your inwardness, which is otherwise utterly inaccessible to me.)

—David Xiao explaining to me that in China the less one shows one's feelings the more one is expressing one's personality.

*

When I sniffed your panties, you laughed, but now and then you ask me if I want to wear your underwear. In 1972 I'd paw through the hamper until I found the dirty, silky drawers of the McGovern campaign volunteer who lived in my family's den. How did my body know to do this?

When I was married, I did the wash a lot. I liked folding Sean's underwear. I liked mating socks. You know what I love? I love taking the lint out of the lint screen. [Madonna]

—Labove, the football-playing school teacher in Faulkner's *The Hamlet*, "wallowing his face against" the plank Eula Varner's been sitting on.

The thing about obsession is, he'll be better off without your ankle. The rest of the week he'll be sniffing the chair where your ankles were. [Susan Cheever]

So it's not that men are pigs. Men are males. [James McManus]

In Maureen Dowd's article about Uma Thurman and the predations of Harvey Weinstein, Quentin Tarantino, and Creative Artists Agency film representatives, the key line (easily overlooked) is, "Her father, Robert Thurman, is a

Buddhist professor of Indo-Tibetan studies at Columbia who thinks Uma is a reincarnated goddess."

That is, will men ever see women as real?

For that to happen, men would first have to get some distance on themselves as vectors on the grid of male sex-drive and understand that their fantasy life is inevitably underwritten by howling weakness. Then they'd have to stop pretending that this weakness is not ever-present.

Antonio Porchia: "Man is weak, and when he makes strength his profession, he is even weaker."

*

Beneath the scatological fixations, one hears the long-postponed vengeance of a child forced to control its bowels, the rage of a grown-up collared by social convention, the exasperation of a householder imprisoned by mate and children. Freudians associate such things as coprophagy with the death instinct, but the familiar obsessions, as they come off here, are so gleefully extravagant—another organ, another fluid, another outrage—that one experiences them, on the contrary, as a desire to embrace life more fully, or at least to embrace talking about life more fully. The comics don't want to do these things; they want to tell about them. The telling is the madness expelled, an act of sanity that allows life to go on.

This is David Denby discussing *The Aristocrats.*

This is so ridiculously wrong I don't know what to say.

The old categories for perversions don't work very well anymore. We need a more subtle approach that can deal with the kind of perversion you find a little bit of in most everyone. [Gerald Fogel]

Perversion can be defined as the sex you like and I don't. [Muriel Dimen]

Oral sex was once seen as a perversion. [Bergner]

We don't choose our desires, and our ability to redirect them is limited. [Kramer]

Inverted Mariolatory is a trope of the French erotic tradition, which endlessly retells the same story of defilement: She who is without sin is submerged by her Lord in a baptismal river of filth to emerge as She who is without shame. [Judith Thurman]

Purity always flirts with defilement. [Kipnis]

—Catherine Millet's voracious appetite for violation in the name of free agency, aggressively seeking what men like to pretend women must be forced to beg for. The most interesting paradox, however, is that Millet's spectacular hubris in telling this story under her own name is an act of self-mortification more hard-core than any in the text. She even seems to be courting, like her namesake, a kind of martyrdom. The postulant, public ridicule that she drains into a ladle and forces herself to swallow with such a show of humility must be particularly galling to a cultivated French palate. What is most thrilling (rather than merely titillating) about *Story of O* is the tension between its radically explicit scenes of torture and fornication and the purity of the sentences that describe them. Dominique Aury's reticent virtuosity—her withholding—is the foil for O's abject self-abandon. If this weren't the case, her fable would be not the masterpiece that it is but a clinical case study of masochism, author's and subject's, in the form of a mildly heretical, comically exalted, didactically perverse, and ultimately banal piece of French art porn, like the volume here under review. [Thurman]

I'm not interested so much in how people survive as in how they avoid humiliation. I think avoiding humiliation is the core of tragedy and comedy and probably of our lives. [John Guare]

Humiliation contains an entire theatrical apparatus, even if only in the minds of the soiled parties—tyrant, victim, witness. [Wayne Koestenbaum]

Humiliation runs like a rash over the body of all of Koestenbaum's/my books (this book being my most self-mortifying by far).

I want the humiliation, the shame. In my soul I believe I am one of the fallen, and my natural and proper condition in the world is that of a man who needs cleansing. I deserve and need to be caught; deserve and need bad reviews; deserve and need to be abused; to get punished. [Gray]

Nathanael West hates himself and postulates a theory that you are always killed by the thing you love, while Ian Fleming loves only himself, his attraction to women, his sexual prowess. [Richard Burton]

We will never tire of hearing about the native sadness behind the construction of glamour. [Daphne Merkin]

Trump's contempt for beautiful women who like to be abused is boundless, and he's full of stories of supermodels, women he might call twelves (not their size), clinging to a rock star's legs and the rock star kicking them away. "You have to treat 'em like shit," Trump has said. [Julie Baumgold]

There is a kind of sexual pleasure in his own vileness, in his very attack on the romantic ideal. [Louis Berger]

On that horrible Thursday morning, Ted wound up as filthy and "forced in upon" as a masochist is likely to find himself. [McManus]

Why, when passing a dazzling woman, do I now look down?

I used to hold eye contact as long as I could.

—the plainer, smarter girl whose obvious need to dominate her peers ensures her rejection. [Merkin]

And/or (which is worse):
excited by the proximity of rejection.

*

You once expressed astonishment that even that wildly unattractive couple over there needs love, can express love, is wildly in love.

When he was fifty-three, John Derek was asked by Barbara Walters whether he would still love his wife, Bo Derek, then twenty-three, if she were disfigured or paralyzed. He thought for a while and demurred. Bo Derek tried hard to smile but couldn't.

When I was thirty-one, I was informed that someone had written, in a stall in the women's bathroom in a bookstore, "David Shields is a great writer and a babe to boot." This is pretty much the high point of my life, when my acne was long gone and I still had hair and was thin without dieting and could still wear contacts and thought I was going to become famous.

What is Bob Balaban, anyway, a professional punching bag? What indignity will the movies not subject him to? What indignity will he not accept? What depth of self-hatred allows him to be used this way? What does it mean to have a face that the camera reviles? Couldn't his life count, too, along with the beautifully real (romantic, operatic, tragic) lives whirling around him? Could he ever see himself in romantic, operatic, tragic terms? What have these roles done to him?

Operatic love—am I myself capable of it?
I would think not.

*

What could possibly have been your motivation to call my uncle (to whom I bear a strong resemblance) "homely"—the frisson you thought I'd feel/just did feel?

My ugliness will set me apart until I die. [Leduc]

At a deeper level I want to disappear, to shrink myself into the carpet's deep pile.

Michel Leiris's attitude is unredeemed by the slightest tinge of self-respect. This lack of esteem or respect for himself is obscene. [Susan Sontag, getting it wrong, as always]

Alone in a hotel room, I will quickly create an area overflowing with garbage.
That area is me.

*

After eating an elegant dinner at a gala or a fancy restaurant or a rich person's house, I'll come home and eat Doritos or Oreos or mint-chip ice cream.
I prefer to eat in the student cafeteria rather than in the faculty club.
Nothing is hotter for me than the porn trope Hot for Teacher (moi as student).
I don't want to even pretend to be high and mighty, which is why I have zero sexual allure in the classroom.
I work in my basement office, with the curtains closed.

*

I'm married to someone who either has nothing or wants nothing, rendering me in possession of nothing.

My first name, "David," means "beloved" in Hebrew. My last name, "Shields," was originally "Schildkraut" until my father changed it after the war. My fate is inscribed in my name: out of who knows what fear, I shield myself from my beloved. A more optimistic interpretation would, of course, see my name indicating that I shield my beloved, or that my beloved shields me, but part of the problem is that such glosses seem to me too glossy.

How did I come to stand so far outside of things?
Was I exiled or did I exile myself?

*

Daddy, I love you.
Silence.
Daddy, I love you.
I love you, too.
You didn't answer the first time.

—my lifelong trouble saying "I" whenever I say "I love you."
"Love you" isn't "I love you."
It's not even close.

Reportedly, we are born to love and be loved.
We are? I don't feel that at all.

Fathers and teachers, I ponder, What is hell? I maintain that it is the suffering of being unable to love. [Dostoevsky]

Jailbreak:
Mickey Rooney said that when he'd go to a party with Marilyn Monroe, by the end of the evening he'd be coveting the gawky girl carrying around the trays of food.
Eroticism, as everyone knows, lies in the flaw: the woman whose blouse doesn't quite match her skirt; the little bulge

of tummy fat; the odd comment; the porn actress with the pimple on her ass.

Once, flipping through the pictures in a dirty magazine, I noticed, on a woman's leg and back, a couple of blotches marked with grease-pencil circles, which, rather than being responded to by the photo retoucher, had, through negligence, remained, like a critique of false premises.

V

—

LIFE IS TRAGIC

(EVERYBODY

KNOWS IT)

The subject heading of an email you wrote to me ten years into our marriage: "The boy in love with bare rooms."

I'm not a person.
I don't know how to be a person.
Or maybe it's just that together we aren't people, exactly.

I don't know how to live.
I don't know, either, but I'm trying.
I don't even know how to try.

I'm afraid.
Don't be.
Basically, at heart, I'm a coward.
Basically, so is everybody.

You should have been a girl.
You should have been a boy.

*

For as long as anyone can remember, American movie actors have been exploring their vulnerable and sensitive sides. Masculine displays of unguarded feeling and agonized introspection may be the norm in serious dramas, but the depiction of genuine male weakness remains something of a taboo. Very few leading men are brave enough to risk appearing cowardly, indecisive, or passive-aggressive, and ordinary men in the audience, observing these traits onscreen, are likely to decline the invitation to identify with them. We would much rather think of ourselves as stoic, fearless, and empathetic, however distant our real selves are from these ideals. The willingness to appear weak—to represent, in other words, a familiar variety of real, contemporary American man—may be Mark Ruffalo's great distinction as an actor. This mixed reaction is only fitting. Mr. Ruffalo's asymmetrical face, with its soft mouth and large, worried eyes, was designed to show ambivalence. [Scott]

Simone de Beauvoir's painstakingly elaborate and elaborated theory: "woman" must "become"; she must, as "subject," actively make herself an object in order to be fulfilled. If she thinks of herself as only an object or believes her mate sees her only as an object, she either forsakes her identity—"denies her humanity"—or feels dominated and humiliated; if she seeks only to be a subject, on the other hand, she'll also be frustrated because strictly as such her desire can't be fulfilled. It's in the ebb and flow between her will and her willful carnality that she becomes a "mature woman." [Mark Eleison]

When asked about her life-long, open relationship with the diminutive, walleyed, hideous Sartre, who had dozens of brief, jealousy-inciting affairs with acolytes (and who, like JFK, would always come almost immediately), de Beauvoir said, "There's theory and there's practice."

We are, I know not how, double within ourselves, with the result that we do not believe what we believe, and we cannot rid ourselves of what we condemn. [Michel de Montaigne]

This talk explores a trenchant feature of the so-called sex wars: the false dichotomy between activism against sexual violence and demands for expanded sexual rights and expression. Egan argues that these debates mark a core conflict within the feminist family narrative. To resolve it, feminists must engage a greater range of affects and the concept of ambivalence. This perspective recognizes disgust/envy as a site of confusion and misdirection but also as a deeply important sphere of insight and knowledge. [flyer for lecture]

I used to think unsolvable ambivalence meant the absence or even end of love; now I think it's the essence of it.

If I had a dollar for every teenage girl who told me she masturbated to a sex scene in *American Psycho* or *Glamorama,* I'd retire. [Bret Easton Ellis]

*

What does a JAP do to her asshole every morning?
Send him to work.
(I don't find JAP jokes funny; I find them hot.)

Much Israeli porn reaches back for its imagery into the Holocaust. Popular symbols, styles, locations, props—trains, showers, dark tunnels, very skinny women, weird doctor-nurse garb—are all straight out of *The Night Porter* (if obliquely so). [Bright]
—the German obsession with scat porn.

A major trope of Japanese porn—this was especially true in the immediate aftermath of World War II—involves a Japanese man slavishly eating out a big, beautiful, buxom, American blonde.

American BDSM sites often feature a black man who is either a couple's stud service or a begrudging, stone-faced submissive.
—Chuck Berry's obsession with shitting on women and women shitting on him.

The submissive tops from the bottom. It's the domina-trix who serves the slave. So many of these guys want to be "forced" to take dick. I remember Lindsay telling me that it was only when she did her first submissive session that she felt like a sex worker. The thrill the women at the Royal Fortress get from being dominant is probably proportionate to their anger at how subjugated they feel in the real world. [Kiku Shuji]

Our flesh arrives to us out of history, like everything else does. We may believe we fuck stripped of social artifice; in bed, we even feel we touch the bedrock of human nature itself. But we are deceived. [Angela Carter]

History never lags.
It lives on our nerve endings.

*

Xantippe is a shrew; living with her teaches me to get along with the rest of the world. [Socrates]
   Really?
   Really?
   That's not how it works at all.

—the cruel woman in furs who will allow him to be her slave . . . his rapturous acquiescence . . . in his conscious guid-ance of both his own and his mistress's will, Severin will have penetrated into the beating heart of a solitary man's most profound desires. [flap copy for Leopold von Sacher-Masoch's novel *Venus in Furs*]

—the terrifying similarity between the unconscious desires of the solitary man and the disruptive needs of the visible world. [Hawkes]

Or as Elizabeth Bowen writes about the protagonist of her novel *The Heat of the Day* (set in London during the Blitz and published in 1948), "She could no more blame the world than one can blame any fellow sufferer: in these last twenty of its and her own years, she had to watch in it what she felt in herself—a clear-sightedly helpless progress toward disaster. The fateful course of her fatalistic century seemed more and more her own."

It begins with them hating you and ends with you hating yourself. [James Baldwin]

I don't understand why I've sought out people already feeling broken by life. What do I mean by "broken"? I mean me.

Why do you cause me more pain than anyone? Which is not really the fight. The fight doesn't even involve you. The fight is with myself, and it's more debate than fight. It's, Why do I like pain so much? The answer has yet to present itself. [Hunt]

You like it when it hurts.

I'm not only always one-down. I'm switchable.
Honey, no.

—attracted to what hates me; indifferent to what loves me.

I didn't come, but maybe that's a good sign, because I can come only if I hate the other person. I've been talking to my online therapist about that. [Lena Dunham]

Hate gets me hard.
Dude, hate gets everybody hard.

*

There were people in the world who were good at love and people who were bad at it. [Lorrie Moore]

I used to think I was the latter and you were the former.
Now I'm not so sure.
What would you say?

I love how sad you seem to be.
I love how sad we are together.
Debbie Downers.
Gloomy Guses.
Eeyores.
The confirmation of each other's misery—is that all it is?

The only scandal is that there is no scandal.
Or: The scandal, for me, is that there is no scandal.
(Eliot Spitzer's only real crime was wearing socks.)

*

An Updike story, published in 1960, called "Wife-Wooing": I love the idea that courtship never ends, because it doesn't. In a way, it's not entirely clear when it begins, either.

Michael Douglas: The embarrassing thing about doing a sex scene is that "this is how you have sex. I mean, this is how you actually do it."

What does "Just Do It" mean exactly? It means: don't think about it; don't offer excuses; don't rationalize ineptitude; ambivalence is for pussies; the contemplative life is one long evasion; mine is not to reason why; but also, clearly, just fuck; don't offer bullshit excuses; the physical life is the only reality; only conscientious objectors retreat to the hospital waiting-room of the mind.

We make love, though that's not quite the right term; it's more like fucking.

You often say, *Nope, sorry, not feeling it,* but then the fucking gets us there.

I keep saying, *You can't rationalize your way to feeling. You can't torque your brain. You have to fool your brain. Your body has to do the feeling, then the feeling follows.* (Hopeful version.)

Unless there's some emotional tie, says Bianca Jagger, I'd rather play tennis.

Jay, the book's narrator, has taken psychic refuge in the idea of a perfect mate, in what symbiosis with such a creature would offer, to the point that he self-protectively ridicules the very kind of union that has become his unattainable grail. Speaking of a friend he names Asif, the emblematic steadfast and loyal spouse, he says, "I recall him describing how much he enjoys sucking her cunt. Apparently he's grunting and slurping down there for hours, after all this time, and wonders whether his soul will only emerge through her ears." Jay's tone is dismissive and mocking, but this ugliness is a defense. What agony to admit that boring and conventional Asif might have found his way to a communion the artistic Jay glorifies. [Harrison]

Say it.
It tastes like heaven.

*

How does one person get, develop, and maintain power over another person?
It's not even that complicated. It's just math.

The sadist identifies, implicitly, with the masochist; how else could the scenarist conjure the scenario so concretely?

All desire objectifies.
There's no such thing as desire without it.
Desire is impersonal, is what I'm trying to say.

Today people tend to think that the point of sex is pleasure, orgasm. But, sincerely, I don't think there's any point to sex at all. People think there's some secret they'll discover in that black box of sex, which will help them live better or make them happy. And in fact there's nothing, nothing, nothing there at all. [Millet]

The individual has a body, and that body is a machine that can be broken down into parts. [Nicole Sault]

Written, with a Sharpie, onto the chest of the male model in an underwear ad on the side of a bus: *Sweet Machine*. [Doty]

The body is a machine that runs on fear. [Greg Iles]

To Carson McCullers, the lover is a wretched creature; the beloved is an indifferent sadist who feels nothing (but contempt). If that's all it is—and I'm pretty sure it is, aren't you?—we're fucked (thank god).

In order to find our bodies funny, we must first become machines, see our bodies as machines. The body is a frail and fallible machine, and I see its mechanics as absurd. We're puppets, occupying moving shapes as a way to symbolize our living questions.

In other words, the sex people have really matters.
So do their sex fantasies.
It all really matters.
It also all really doesn't matter.
And yet, of course—

*

Nobody passes up romance. [Michaels]

Girls like to be spanked. [Michaels]

I like the roughness sometimes. [Matthews]

There's no romance without female masochism. [Carter]

My work cuts like a steel blade at the base of a man's penis. [Carter]

I have always found it hard to feel sexual desire without some sense of superiority. [Graham Greene]

I would just say, There's no romance without masochism. What's my point?

Someone must be suffering, is all.

*

Love calls us to the things of this world. [Richard Wilbur]

Love is a long close scrutiny. [Hawkes]

The desires of the heart are as crooked as corkscrews. [W. H. Auden]

Love is the crooked thing. [William Butler Yeats]

Your problem is you're not happy being sad, but that's what love is. [John Carney]

Love is sadness. [Antonya Nelson]

This is the saddest story. [Ford]

Life is tragic.

Everybody knows it.

Especially you (which is what connects us).

In Jill Alexander Essbaum's first novel, when the protagonist asks her husband what the purpose of pain is, he says, "Pain is the proof of life."

*

I found myself at the threshold of the terrifying enigma that is another human being: [Dobb]

I'm so moved by the hacked nudes of Jennifer Lawrence, Kate Upton, Victoria Justice, Jessica Brown Findlay, Mary Elizabeth Winstead, Kaley Cuoco, Jill Scott, Yvonne Strahovski, et al. What a relief. Posing, these women are as sad and afraid and shy—above all, shy—about sex as we are. They're "sex symbols," but they're embarrassed by the subject, too.

Human kind cannot / Bear very much reality. [Eliot]
We can tolerate even less the loneliness that comes from not actually seeing each other.

Isn't sex supposed to be free, easy? What's wrong with me that I resist? Why do I feel so afraid of the surrender, the sexual depths? [Tisdale]
Or: What's wrong with me? What am I afraid of? I'm ashamed of what I desire. I'm most ashamed of the shame itself.

He wants what everyone wants, some version of it, anyway—to be held, to hold, to be hit or to hit, to pin or to be pinned, to be entered and exited, to be turned inside out with lust and longing or longing and lust, up or down, or up and then down, some version of the sadomasochism that is at the center of most sexual desire, but he's not going to admit it to me, and maybe not even to himself. [Lauren Slater]

—the sexual shyness that, over time, has developed between you and me; the brief flare, several years ago, when we were obsessed with each other again for a few weeks . . .

When we make love, as much as everyone wants to come and see stars and feel the world turn, we resist intense sexual experience more than we embrace it. It's very difficult for us to let go. [Bright]

—you waiting until it showed up, briefly and obliquely, on a *Sex and the City* episode to tell me exactly what you like.

Mr. Watson, come here. I want to see you.
Ha ha.
Darling, face me.

*

If you like to be sucked or bitten and I like to suck or bite you, we may enjoy each other. [Silvan Tomkins]

But if both of us like to be bitten, then we can do nothing (except fight, which neither of us enjoys, about who has to do the biting this time). Whereas if both of us like to bite, we can still bite each other or compete, which is fun for us! The only combination that can't possibly work (believe me, I've tried) is two bottoms. Two bottoms: tragedy. Two tops: momentary happiness. Top and bottom: perfect happiness. [Aaron Kunin]

It was around this time that I first had the thought: we fuck well because he is a passive top and I am an active bottom. [Maggie Nelson]

Our sexual inclinations align.

*

Mister is loving.
Deester is sweet.
D is neutral.
David means you're mad.

I love when you say, *Hey, you*; call me *Shields* (guy talk); or, especially, when you say, *You're not so bad*, then push me—hard.

By far my favorite look of yours is when you put your hands on your hips and pretend to be quite angry but are actually kidding and happy and playful, even loving.

Briefly, I relax.

*

I reach for you. You lean away from me. It is like falling.

You once said something to the effect that you weren't sure what was keeping us together other than our daughter. You weren't saying this in a nasty way—just that (at least superficially) we're so dissimilar in our personalities, our friends, our activities. It literally baffled us a bit as to why we were together, and honestly I think it still baffles us. Sometimes I wonder, rather idly, what other people think connects us.

Women consistently rate "best-smelling" the T-shirts from men whose immune systems contain important components that theirs lack. A woman is drawn to a man whose immune system makes up for whatever is lacking in hers, thus ensuring that their offspring would have a robust defense system. However, couples who share interests are more likely to have successful marriages than those who don't. Thus, we are caught in a complex bind, when it comes to marriage— drawn (in order to create healthy offspring) toward partners who deeply differ from us, and then, once the offspring have sprung, we are left with a partner who may be more foreign than friend. What is one to do in such a situation? Say, simply, Please, and hope that single, simple word ferries you and your partner to some simple place where you can stitch your strings together? [Slater]

So is that what you think—that we live parallel lives, that we never really meet? Is that what your experience tells you? And if so, is difference such a bad thing? If there were no difference, what would become of desire?

Driving through the Alps with friends. . . . The beauty of this area amazes me. . . . Mountains and water—so green and blue that only Italian could describe them. . . . And the black gray of the tanks that appear quickly as we move through the switchbacks. . . . Europe never lets me forget that everyone is different from everyone else on the planet, and this difference is both lovely and awful. [Samantha Ruckman]

Agnès Jaoui's *The Taste of Others* is the smartest, saddest movie about sex ever made. Clara, asked by her student what the most difficult part of acting is, says, "To depend on another's desire." Valerie, surprised that she's going out with Fred, says, "I would have never guessed it. We have nothing in common." When Clara says about someone who likes her and the play in which she's starring, "I don't like his kind," her friend Manie asks, "Is there anybody you like?" The film, which is also known as *It Takes All Kinds*, knows that what we love and hate about other people is how different they are from us: we're disgusted by this difference, and we're excited by it.

*

Among the hundreds of Love Lab questions I've just answered, this one question won't leave my mind—something about whether I "have started to imagine/wish that my partner is dead or been killed." A classic—not to mention common—response with couples (totally "normal," "healthy," "average" couples) for whom despite the existence of legal divorce, it somehow seems more optimal if the other person would just go ahead and die or get riddled with some fast-moving disease. Charming, right? It's not that I wish him dead. It's just that somehow death looks easier. Life would decide for us. And if it were some disease, I could get focused on helping him leave the earth in a loving and thoughtful way and I could feel really good about myself—how kind and amazing and above it all I am. More importantly, it would save me from having to choose. So yes, goddamnit, even though I've never uttered this aloud, the Gottmans have read my mind. And what's better (or worse) is that they're telling me that my possibly imagining my husband getting accidentally caught in the wood chipper or tripping on some old land-mine wire while touring Vietnam is (apparently) totally normal and utterly healthy marital behavior. I can't decide if this should comfort me or prompt me to take a vow of singlehood for the rest of my life. If I've got this straight, the Gottmans are telling me that married couples everywhere are out there envisioning their husbands/wives being pushed in front of fast-moving trains or falling into fatally scalding mineral pools in Yellowstone National Park or nursing them through a rare, flesh-eating disease. This is normal. This is marriage. And the Gottmans assure me that even some of those couples actually make it. Is our species a wreck or what? [I can't, for the life of me, figure out where I saw this or who said it, but it rings true, don't you think?]

*

Do all your films have a common theme?

The only theme I can think of is really a question: Why can't people be happier together? [Akira Kurosawa, Q&A with Donald Richie]

I'm a huge fan of a TV episode (can't recall the name of the brief-lived and actually rather anodyne show, from the late eighties) in which a couple goes away for the weekend in order to try to have a romantic weekend at a secluded mountain cabin, where everything, of course, feels forced; only, later, in the harsh fluorescence of a 7-Eleven—surrounded by beef jerky and porn magazines—do they fall in love again.

I've never cried harder or longer in my life.

I dearly/desperately want a real marriage—whatever that means. I think it means two people standing before each other completely naked; does such a thing exist? I don't know, but in opposition to that essay we read in praise of a marriage made of masks, I still want it (the unmasking).

Do you love this book? Do you hate it? Will it mark the end of our marriage? The beginning of it? Putative (true?) goal for this book: a greater intimacy (at a minimum, candor?) between us.

The nicest thing you've ever said to me (admittedly, this was an eternity ago—on the inside of a card on our third anniversary):

What you think of as your weakness I think of as your vulner-ability, which I love.

21st CENTURY ESSAYS

David Lazar and Patrick Madden, Series Editors

This series from Mad Creek Books is a vehicle to discover, publish, and promote some of the most daring, ingenious, and artistic nonfiction. This is the first and only major series that announces its focus on the essay—a genre whose plasticity, timelessness, popularity, and centrality to nonfiction writing make it especially important in the field of nonfiction literature. In addition to publishing the most interesting and innovative books of essays by American writers, the series publishes extraordinary international essayists and reprint works by neglected or forgotten essayists, voices that deserve to be heard, revived, and reprised. The series is a major addition to the possibilities of contemporary literary nonfiction, focusing on that central, frequently chimerical, and invariably supple form: The Essay.